POSITIVE QUOTES for Women

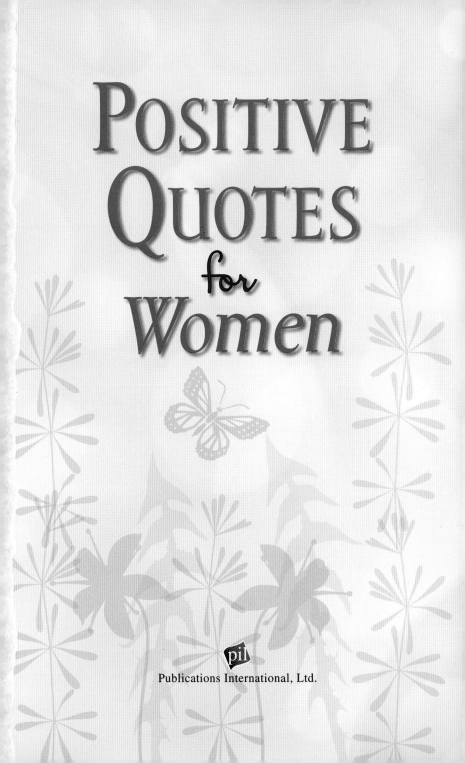

pil

Publications International, Ltd.

Marie D. Jones is the author of several best-selling nonfiction books and a contributing author to numerous inspirational books, including *A Mother's Daily Prayer Book, When You Lose Someone You Love: A Year of Comfort,* and six books from the Echoes of Love series: *Mother, Grandmother, Sisters, Friends, Graduation,* and *Wedding.* To learn more about Jones, visit her website at www.mariedjones.com.

Natalie Walker Whitlock is the author of 13 books, including *A Parent's Guide to the Internet,* and more than 500 articles. She lives with her husband and seven children in Arizona.

Louis Weber, CEO
Publications International, Ltd.
7373 North Cicero Avenue
Lincolnwood, Illinois 60712

ISBN-13: 978-1-4058-6263-9
ISBN-10: 1-4058-6263-2

Manufactured in China.

8 7 6 5 4 3 2 1

Library of Congress Control Number: 2012949823

Bright Side Up Ahead!

While it's not always easy, focusing on the positive in life makes all the difference in the world. Whether facing small frustrations, such as oversleeping or bad traffic, or bigger things, like mistakes at work or— worst of all—a trauma befalling us or a loved one, keeping our cool and staying as positive as possible can make an immeasurable difference.

Let's take the easy example of oversleeping. What choice do we have, in terms of our reaction to this circumstance? We can beat ourselves up and be so upset that we are nearly frozen in our tracks, or we can focus on the positive, take a deep breath, and just shift into fast forward in our routine.

We can apply this approach to the larger issues of big mistakes or shocking accidents. While keeping a positive attitude cannot undo mistakes or roll back time to prevent accidents, it can help us recover and heal more quickly. If we let the incident control and define us, we stay frozen in time with no soothing remedy. If we tap into positive advice, however, we heal—

and we grow in wisdom from the struggles we have overcome. We feel a shift in our mood, our thoughts, and our words, and suddenly, we are thinking in a whole new way, one that motivates and inspires us. Answers and solutions appear where we thought there were none. We feel empowered!

Use *Positive Quotes for Women* as a resource in your daily life. It carries within it the power of words, which can lift us above any fray and help us regain our perspective. From this higher vantage point, we can see the bigger picture, which is a beautiful one. Each entry in this book opens with an inspiring quote, which is followed by a reflection. Each entry ends with an action step that applies the quote and reflection to daily life. On tough days you may find yourself clutching this book, while on great days you may quickly read an entry just for pleasure. Either way, be sure to stay on the bright side—and treasure every moment of your unique life journey.

Mostly Sunny

"If you count the sunny and the cloudy days of the whole year, you will find that the sunshine predominates."

Ovid

―――

Why is it so easy to focus on bad news? Too often it seems that we are focusing on what we are afraid of or what we despise instead of what we love and what makes us happy. What is the use in that? We should immerse ourselves in love and joy, never mind the "other stuff."

For the next few days, I will make it a point to avoid bad news, gossip, and negativity. The forecast for my life is sunny.

Dreams Make All Things Possible

"Dreams are necessary to life."
Anaïs Nin

A life without dreams is like a droopy bouquet. Dreams give depth, vibrancy, texture, and perspective to our "daily grind" and keep us focused on the big picture.

Today I will do one thing to bring me closer to the culmination of a personal dream. Perhaps I will start a chapter of that book I've longed to write or begin training for that 5k.

Your Own Special Song

"If I'm going to sing like someone else,
then I don't need to sing at all."
Billie Holiday

*L*ike snowflakes and fingerprints, all people
are different. Why would you want
to be anyone other than who you are? What
makes you unique is that special song only
you can sing, and it is a song unlike any other.
When combined, all of our individual songs
come together in one splendid chorus. So sing—
loud and proud!

**Today I will express myself authentically at
every opportunity.**

Stay Calm

"Keep cool and you command everybody."
Louis Leon de Saint-Just

When I am having a difficult day, it's so easy for me to lose my temper. And once I lose my temper, things only get worse from there. Funny how when I take a deep breath, retain control, and act from a place of strength, I get things done.

When I encounter challenges today, I will stop and count to ten before I react with anger, frustration, or annoyance. I will stay in command!

Hold Your Head High

"Seek respect mainly from thyself,
for it comes first from within."
Steven H. Coogler

Sometimes we can be our own worst enemies. We wander about, concerned about what others are thinking of us. What really matters, though, is what we think about ourselves. If I truly treasure the creature that I am—the same way I treasure all those I love—others will sense it and respond with respect.

Today I will walk with my head held high.
I know I am not inferior to anyone.

Fleeting Concerns

"When you consider things like stars, our affairs don't seem to matter very much, do they?"
Virginia Woolf

ow often do we lose perspective by focusing on the trivial, annoying

details of life? I think most of us have had this experience: After a "bad" day, we catch sight of some natural beauty by happenstance and find ourselves magically renewed. Life is about focusing on the beautiful and the fulfilling and letting go of the silly and constraining.

The next time I find myself feeling overwhelmed, I will seek out nature and immerse myself in it for a half hour.

Expand the Good

"Little progress can be made by merely attempting to repress what is evil. Our great hope lies in developing what is good."

Calvin Coolidge

———✦———

I find it so easy to see the faults in other people—and in myself. I turn on the nightly news, and it's filled with examples of people treating each other terribly. It is easy to feel outdone. The above words, though, ask us to spread the good so it overtakes the bad. What a hopeful, inspiring tactic!

Today I will do my part to spread the good, whether by doing something as simple as disposing of a piece of trash that I come upon or something bigger, like volunteering at a soup kitchen or as a tutor.

Work Inspires

"Inspiration usually comes during work, rather than before it."

Madeleine L' Engle

⤆

*O*ften the easier path is to sit around and wait for a lightbulb to go off before deciding what road to pursue. The truth is,

though, that usually we need to just begin before any bright ideas really come to us. We must get to work *before* things can start falling into place.

Today I will start working on a project that I've been putting off. I will go back to school, start on that quilt, or begin a sketch for a painting. How great it will feel to finally make progress!

Taking Stock of Priorities

"True wisdom lies in gathering the precious things out of each day that goes by."

E. S. Bouton

Some days, we get so consumed by our activities that we forget why we ever scheduled them in the first place! Are they even all that important? Are we prioritizing trivial matters over things that are more precious in the long run? We must slow down and take stock now and then so we will not overlook what's precious.

Before I go to bed tonight, I will make a list of three things that made me happy today and three things I could have done without. If I make a point to do this once a week, and then act on it, I will have my priorities completely straight before I know it!

Seize Opportunities

"Ride the tributaries to reach the sea."
Arabian Proverb

*U*sually, achieving big goals involves many small steps rather than one big leap. We need to have patience and perseverance. When

we call to mind the big feats in history, there were likely many points leading up to these achievements when the major players could have become discouraged and given up. If the end goal is worth it, we must do whatever it takes to achieve it.

Today I will contemplate my big goal and take at least one small step toward it.

Be Picky

*"One cannot collect all the beautiful
shells on the beach."*
Anne Morrow Lindbergh

*M*ost of us, at some point in our lives, feel
dazzled at the thought of "having it all":
the great job, loving and perfect relationships,
vibrant health,
a marvelous
home...the list
goes on. Perhaps
at times we may
seem to have it
all—or we may
know people
who seem to
have it all. Most
of us, though,
must learn to
be content with
the few gems
life throws to us.
That may sound
defeatist, but the

fact of the matter is, we learn and grow wise by *not* getting what we want. Perhaps one of the "beautiful shells" isn't quite right for us at this point in our lives. It is good to be okay with that and appreciate the beautiful shells we *do* have in our lives. Even one gem is all we really need—as long as it's the perfect one for us.

If I find myself faced with disappointment today, I will get happy by calling to mind the gems of my life.

What We Control

"There is only one path to happiness, and that is cease worrying about things which are beyond the power of our will."

Epictetus

——————

Many of us waste so much of our time worrying about things that are beyond our control. The economy? Vote your conscience and find and maintain the best job you can, and you have done your part. Poverty? Don't overindulge yourself and regularly donate time or money to a local soup kitchen or food depository, and your part is done. Inconsiderate drivers? Send positive vibes their way (they obviously need them!) and move on.

Today I will mind my part in this life, and it will be enough.

Rewarded with Truth

"I tore myself away from the safe comfort of certainties through my love for the truth; and truth rewarded me."

Simone de Beauvoir

Often the truth in a situation is not what we would expect—or even want—it to be. As we mature through experience, we become more comfortable with this uncertainty. It need not make us lose heart. If we do not expect things to be a certain way, we will not be as discouraged when they turn out differently. How often in life are we misled by authority figures, the media, or even each other? Even worse, how often do we lie to ourselves to avoid or deny what we think will be too painful to face? In the long run, the truth always catches up to us, and peace usually comes along with it.

Today I will be truthful in all my interactions with others—and especially with myself.

Peace Inside

"People say to me so often, Jane, how can you be so peaceful when everywhere around you people want books signed, people are asking these questions and yet you seem peaceful,' and I always answer that it is the peace of the forest that I carry inside."

Jane Goodall

*I*t seems that some people are able to seemingly easily get to that "happy place" inside, even in the most stressful situation. Maybe we just need to find that one aspect of life that gives us that peace. For some it might be contemplating a favorite natural scene; for others it might be thinking about loved ones, for still others it might be religion. Whatever it is, figure out what yours is—and keep it at the ready!

Today I will select a happy scene, and I will set my mind on it if I find myself getting stressed.

In Praise of Efficiency

"Nature uses as little as possible of anything."
Johannes Kepler

Waste not, want not; keep it green; reuse and recycle...we hear messages every day about how we need to stop wasting our resources and treat our planet with respect. I sometimes marvel at the amount of trash my family alone creates each week. Animals surely leave little true mess behind. They are prime examples of how to live a greener life.

Today will be a true green day for me. I will use only as much water as is truly necessary, and I will reflect upon every item I throw in the trash. Perhaps in the days to come I can do things a little differently to keep from creating quite so much garbage.

An Abundance of Pardons

"As we grow in wisdom, we pardon more freely."
Madame de Stael

⟶

*M*any of us can think of a time when we held a grudge or harbored resentment for an extended period of time. But as we get older and wiser, we realize that the more positivity we send out, the more we get in return. Soon we find ourselves surrounded by positivity. Grudges and resentments keep us chained in an ugly place, while quick pardons free the other person—and ourselves.

Today I will find time to reflect on my relationships. If there is someone I need to forgive (or if I need forgiveness from another) I will make amends, then bask in the peace.

The Necessities of Life

"Give me love and work—these two only."
William Morris

When most people look at their lives and take stock of what they treasure, they point to their close relationships (love) and meaningful work as the things they find most fulfilling. When we think about it, we could do without just about everything else. As long as we have something to keep us busy and someone to keep us company, our lives feel complete.

Today I will take pride in my work and show my loved ones how much I appreciate them.

Choose to Smile

"The happiest people seem to be those who have no particular reason for being so except that they are so."

William R. Inge

he older I get, the more I realize that being happy is a choice. I can get up every morning and be grumpy and focus on what's wrong, or I can take a deep, soul-filling breath and choose to smile and focus on the good. It is surprising how much light one smile can carry through the world.

Today I will go out into the world with a smile on my face. I will spread the happiness.

Happiness for Others

"It was disappointing to lose the gold, but it meant a lot more to me that my brother won the gold medal. There is more to life than personal goals."

Jackie Joyner-Kersee

Sometimes we get so caught up in our own goals that we forget that our loved ones have their own goals as well. Being generous with our loved ones helps them, and it helps us grow too. By taking the focus off ourselves from time to time, we learn and experience new things that give us an expanded insight on life.

Today I will seize an opportunity to cheer on someone else.

Positive Peace

*"Peace is not the absence of conflict
but the presence of creative alternatives
for responding to conflict."*
Dorothy Thompson

———

I love the idea of world peace as much as the next person, but I often feel pessimistic about the possibility of it. I wonder if we humans are capable of handling conflict without resorting to violence. It is helpful and productive to think of having certain structures in place to promote peace rather than working to get rid of all sources of conflict. Life is conflict. It is how we choose to work through conflict that determines what kind of society we are. If we emphasize what makes us similar to others—instead of what makes us different—I do believe peace is possible.

Today if conflict arises, I will remind myself of the common ground I share with the other person. Focusing on that will help me find a way to resolve the small obstacle we have encountered in our relationship. I will not fuel any small fire by adding anger, defensiveness, or overreaction to it.

An Inside Job

"They can conquer, who believe they can."
William Dryden

⸺

I think most of us have attempted new things in different ways. It is true that when we face a task with confidence and tranquility, things tend to go more smoothly, while if we are afraid and approach something tentatively, our fears tend to get realized. If there is something we truly want to accomplish, we can begin by boldly taking that first step. Success in anything is truly an inside job.

Today I will not be afraid. What is there to lose? I have prepared, and I will prevail.

The Most Important Orders

Simone Weil

48

*H*eroes are not people who merely boss others around. Before they can productively lead others, heroes must first fully command themselves. Heroes ask nothing of others that they wouldn't undertake themselves.

I will strive to be a true hero today by giving a good example to those around me.

Walking Your Talk

"Wisdom does not show itself so much in precept as in life—in firmness of mind and mastery of appetite. It teaches us to do as well as to talk; and to make our words and actions all of a color."

Seneca

When I was growing up, my grandparents always talked to me about integrity. It wasn't until they used the phrase "walking your talk," however, that I really grasped the concept. Being wise is having your words match your actions in all that you do so that you trust yourself and can be trusted by others. Wisdom

also does certainly have to do with "firmness of mind," as I know that when I was younger and less experienced, I would waver more when making decisions, while now I feel sure rather quickly; I rarely second-guess myself.

Today I will make sure I am walking my talk and maintaining integrity in all my interactions.

Pushing Through Fear

"I've been absolutely terrified every moment of my life—and I've never let it keep me from doing a single thing I wanted to do."

Georgia O'Keeffe

Life is scary, if we really think about it (or perhaps overthink about it!). Even "good" days hold moments of worry or uncertainty, but that uncertainty is what keeps each day new and exciting. If we let fear hold us back, we will miss out on so many wonderful experiences. Sure, we may lose or end up hurt, but we also may win or experience utter joy. So much of life is about just moving forward. If you let fear hold you back, you will never know what dreams you could have achieved.

If I find myself feeling afraid today, I will stand firm and push through the fear.

Be Happy

"Most people are about as happy as they make up their minds to be."

Abraham Lincoln

The most magnetic people are not necessarily the most good-looking, famous, or accomplished. They are the ones who always seem to be happy, no matter what might be going on in their lives. They spread joy and happiness wherever they go. When they encounter troubles, instead of being angry, they keep smiling and come up with a solution.

Today I choose to be happy. No matter what happens, I will keep smiling.

Shared Meals

"When poets write about food it is usually celebratory. Food as the thing-in-itself, but also the thoughtful preparation of meals, the serving of meals, meals communally shared: a sense of the sacred in the profane."

Joyce Carol Oates

$\mathcal{S}$ome of my fondest childhood memories revolve around my grandmother working in the kitchen to prepare dinner for the extended family on special occasions. For her, it was never a chore—it was a way to show her gratitude for having been blessed with so many loved ones. She beamed with pride as she presented and served the meal. The food was a reflection of her love for all of us.

Today I will plan a menu for a wonderful meal and arrange a gathering to share it.

Meaningful Work

"For me, work represents the
supreme luxury of life."
Albert M. Greenfield

$\mathcal{B}$emoaning, at times, the drudgery involved in work and wanting time to pursue our own interests and activities is understandable, but without meaningful work, life can easily seem devoid of purpose. So whatever our work is—whether it is tending to crops, keeping up a home and looking after a

family, or working in a factory or office—it is good to take pride in it as our own and perform it to the best of our ability.

As I work today, I will reflect on what a treasure work is and contemplate ways I can improve my performance.

Eyes of Love

"Love isn't blind. It's only love that sees."
Sarah Orne Jewett

*T*here are generally two ways to approach any person or situation: one is from a critical standpoint, and the other is from a loving standpoint. Many people call love blind because they see someone acting out of love as acting without regard to reason. Love does not always seem reasonable, that is true. Love tends to see things as they should be rather than as they actually are. A person who always acts out of love is always shooting for the best rather than working from a place of fear or self-protection. Promoting love is more important than protecting our own egos, though, because it is the only way any ideal can ever be achieved.

Today I will put my love goggles on and see everything around me from a standpoint of love.

Bask in the Simplicity

*"Life is really simple, but men insist
on making it complicated."*
Confucius

 food? Check. Clothing? Check. Shelter?
Check. Someone to love? Check. Anything
beyond these is pretty much gravy, but it is

easy to get so caught up in accumulating and acquiring that this piece of wisdom gets left behind in the dust. Sure, some of the extras (transportation, entertainment) verge on being essentials; throw in a couple of extras to spice things up, then survey your life and smile.

Today I will make an effort to live as simply as possible.

Let Your Inner Artist Out

*"The only thing I know is that I paint because
I need to, and I paint whatever passes through
my head without any consideration."*

Frida Kahlo

Many of us have something we "need"
to do, whether it's painting, writing,
singing, or any of many other creative pursuits.
It is the activity that centers us, that anchors
us and helps us make sense of things when life
gets crazy. When we feel the urge to be active
in this way, we should not resist it. How much
happier might we be if we allowed our inner
artist out from time to time?

**The next time I have an urge to create, I will
follow where the urge leads.**

The Highest Heights

"If I accept you as you are, I will make you worse; however, if I treat you as though you are what you are capable of becoming, I help you become that."

Johann Wolfgang von Goethe

*H*aving a lot expected of us is good for us. If no one expects much of us, it is easier to just be satisfied with meeting low or average expectations. If a lot is expected of us, however, we may not reach the highest heights, but we will likely climb

quite high. This does not mean we should be treated terribly if we fail—it just means we try our best and we encourage others to try their best at all times as well.

Today I will reach for the highest heights in all my endeavors, and I will encourage those around me to do the same.

Shocked into Amusement

"Perhaps one has to be very old before one learns to be amused rather than shocked."

Pearl S. Buck

*S*hock should be reserved for truly awful or harmful things like tragic events or horrible crimes. When it comes to relatively harmless things like differing opinions or edgy fashions or art, it is good to take them in stride and with a smile, if possible. When we react with shock to minor things, it is a sign of inexperience and perhaps taking ourselves too seriously. Not everything is about us. We should take pride in the fact that we live in a free society where we are all allowed to express ourselves in any way we see fit—as long as our actions do not cause harm to others, of course. Life is unpredictable; sometimes, you have to just sit back and smile at the craziness of it all.

Today if I find myself feeling shocked by relatively harmless things, I will try to find the humor in the situation and have a good, stress-relieving laugh about it.

Communication Is Key

"There is always hope when people are forced to listen to both sides."

John Stuart Mill

I am grateful to live in a society where we are innocent until proven guilty. Sometimes in my own life I find myself rushing to judgment, whether over gossip about an acquaintance or a perceived slight by a friend. It is easy to judge or feel miffed and wallow in self-pity. The stronger, safer route, though, is to wait and see what transpires and talk to

all parties instead of devoting a lot of energy to initial knee-jerk emotions. Once I listen to all sides, I may be relieved to find that things were not at all as they first seemed.

If I find myself rushing to judgment today, I will take things slowly and reflect. I will take into account both sides of the situation instead of immediately jumping to a one-sided conclusion.

Words and Pictures

"We write to taste life twice, in the moment, and in retrospection."

Anaïs Nin

———

*L*ike most people these days, I have a camera on my cell phone, and I often snap pictures of treasured people and experiences. But pictures don't capture all the details of memories in the making. So I also journal daily, as a way of making permanent notes of everything I am feeling. That way I can go back and read about what happened and what I did, and experience it all for the second time from a different viewpoint. It is truly thrilling and beautiful to go back over my experiences 10, even 20, years later. Sometimes things are exactly as I remember them, but other times, I marvel at the thoughts and views of that younger version of myself.

Tonight I will write about what I experienced today, for even "typical" days often contain amazing moments to be treasured and shared.

Finding My Part

*"I am only one, but still I am one;
I cannot do everything, but still I can
do something; and because I cannot
do everything I will not refuse to do
the something that I can do."*

Edward E. Hale

---

*M*any of the challenges we face today are huge and seem insurmountable. It is important to remember, though, that those who came before us surmounted challenges as big or bigger than those we face today. It comes down to each person doing his or her part until a tipping point is reached and true change occurs.

Today I will do something to improve the world around me, whether it's volunteering in some capacity, giving money to a reputable charity, or writing to my representative about a local issue.

Expand Your Horizons

*"Life never becomes a habit to
me. It's always a marvel."*
Katherine Mansfield

Most of us find comfort and safety in
leading scheduled, predictable lives. It
is good to step out on a limb once in a while,
though, to get as much as we can out of life.
New experiences enliven our existence and help
us to grow as individuals.

**Today I will seek out something delightful.
Perhaps I will venture out to a nearby area
that I have always been too busy to explore.**

We Are in Control

"You must learn to be still in the midst of activity and to be vibrantly alive in repose."
Indira Gandhi

Discipline is very important in this life. Things will come at us that we are not expecting, but as we grow older, wiser, and more experienced, we must cultivate that inner strength that steers our lives. If we are at a large, frenetic party but feel the need to opt out for a moment and reflect, we need to mentally be able to do that. In the reverse, if we are enjoying a little "alone time" but feel energized to study or figure out a solution to a current problem, we need to be able to be active mentally. Whatever we need to focus on at any given time, we can accomplish it through practice and discipline.

Today I am in control. Whatever my needs are, I will be in tune with them. I will operate from a place of power within me.

The Limits of Love

"Nobody has ever measured, not even poets, how much the heart can hold."

Zelda Fitzgerald

Certain actions can be baffling. The first examples that come to my mind are the stories of crime victims' families forgiving the criminals. In the past this has left me speechless. Part of me was aghast because the criminals seemed so undeserving. But where the intellect cannot even see a way around the pain, the heart is still able to act out of love. Instead of clinging to that anger and hate, you expand your heart and let the destructive feelings go. What a beautiful testament to the lost loved ones—the last act in their honor is a beautiful one from the heart.

Today when I am challenged to be angry, upset, or disappointed, I will try to love just a little bit more.

Choose to Grow

*"The strongest principle of growth
lies in human choice."*
George Eliot

Every day we are faced with choices. The harder ones lead to growth, while the easier ones lead nowhere. We can choose to stay where we are, or we can choose to grow. Growth can be scary and uncertain, but it can also be beautiful and wonderful. We just have to be brave and make the difficult choice.

Today, if faced with a choice, I will take the challenging path full of growth.

One Courageous Package

"I belong to no race nor time. I am the eternal feminine with its string of beads."

Zora Neale Hurston

Women are such amazing forces in the world. We are the bearers and nurturers of life, the mediators and diplomats, the mothers and daughters and sisters and friends, the compassionate hearts and fierce warrior goddesses—all in one courageous package. One thing I love about being a woman is that sense of sisterhood with other women. We share the bond of womanhood and all the possibilities it represents.

Today I will be conscious of my feminine strengths and talents, and I will put them to good use.

Live Out Your Destiny

"To be what we are, and to become what we are capable of becoming, is the only end of life."
Robert Louis Stevenson

W hat's it all for? Most people come back to that question repeatedly throughout their lives. Human beings yearn for meaning. Being true to your own essence and making the

most of your talents and abilities seems like the simplest answer, and it is a realistic one as well. We get this amazing chance to shine, so let's not let it pass us by. We don't have to be the wealthiest, most beautiful person in the world—we just each have to make the most of our unique talents and circumstances.

Today I will be in tune with myself, and I will push myself to accomplish as much as possible.

Equal Footing

Civilization means different things to different people. Some people seem to think it means being as far removed from animals and nature as possible (so much so that we hardly seem a part of nature anymore), while others think it means maintaining a certain order and level of decency. Though the civilization we live in is far from achieving equal respect for all people, we can make progress every day, and I can certainly encourage progress in my own community.

If I notice a wrong today, I will work to make it right. Perhaps if I encounter a homeless person I will buy him a meal, or I will donate my time or money to a cause that helps people who are less fortunate than I am.

In Tune with the Mysterious

"The most beautiful thing we can experience is the mysterious. It is the source of all art and science."
Albert Einstein

*L*ong before the days of mind-boggling technology and endless gadgets, children had few things to do besides play outside, explore the woods, or look for shells on the beach. The world seemed filled with wonder and mystery. That mystery is still there now, of course. We just have to slow down and notice it.

Today I will take a moment and remove myself from the distractions of technology. I will stand in awe of something natural and far removed from my daily routine.

Start Today

"If we are ever to enjoy life, now is the time—not tomorrow, nor the next year, nor in some future life after we have died. The best preparation for a better life next year is full, complete, harmonious, joyous life this year.... Today should always be our most wonderful day."

Thomas Dreier

ometimes we say things like, "Tomorrow I will start an exercise program," or "Tomorrow I will make that overdue call to my cousin," or "Tomorrow I will look for better work." Why not start improving your life right now—this very moment? When we choose to put things off, it only gets easier to choose to put them off again the next day, and on and on. Do something today. It can be as little as taking a quick morning walk, making a short call while fixing dinner, or sending one brief networking e-mail. If you start this minute, you can be energized and inspired by tangible progress sooner rather than later.

Today I will make progress—however small—on a situation that has been causing me stress.

92

Take It All In

*"The true traveler is he who goes on foot, and
even then, he sits down a lot of the time."*
Colette

*Y*ou must immerse yourself in a place to
really get to know it. You could live in a
city for years but
not really know its
fullness because
you drive your car
everywhere and
stick to the same
routine—work,
home, favorite
restaurant, favorite
store, home again,
repeat. Travelers go

to other places to experience them, but if you rush around and don't take the time to really observe, you will miss a lot of the details that set a place apart.

Today I will travel to a new destination, even someplace close to home that I have never noticed. I will take my time, step out of my protective routine, and take in the fullness of my surroundings.

Slow Down

"There is more to life than increasing its speed."
Mohandas K. Gandhi

---

*C*ell phones, tablets, laptops, and gadgets galore—sometimes you can feel like you are nothing but a terminal in an electronic network! The world has become a place where everything must be faster, cheaper, smaller, and easier. Maybe that is why so many of us feel breathless and worn out! Slow down, turn

off the electronics, and take stock of your surroundings. Start really living your life—before it passes you by.

Today I will do without the distractions of modern technologies whenever possible. I will take the day slow and easy and relish every little wonder I come across.

Reach, Stretch, Grow!

"This became a credo of mine: Attempt the impossible in order to improve your work."

Bette Davis

*P*ush yourself, and you're bound to grow. Attempt the impossible, and even if you fall short, you're still beyond where you were

yesterday. "Failure" is not a bad thing in this case. If you reach, you grow—even if you fail to achieve your ultimate goal. And you can always reach again tomorrow. Reach, stretch, grow. Reach, stretch, grow. One of these days, you just might get there. And if you don't, you at least achieved significant growth, which is sure to have improved your performance.

Today I will push myself, and I will grow.

The World in a Flower

"When you take a flower in your hand and really look at it, it's your world for the moment. I want to give that world to someone else."

Georgia O'Keeffe

Whether it's wildflowers in the springtime, dandelions in the hands of a toddler, or a dozen roses delivered on your anniversary—flowers have an amazing and singular appeal! They are things of wonder, and we never tire of them. The thought (or picture!) of them has the power to make us smile long after the flowers themselves have drooped.

Today I will brighten a loved one's day by giving them flowers.

Nothing to Fear

"Our doubts are traitors and make us lose the good we often might win, by fearing to attempt."
Jane Addams

What might we do today, if we brushed off any fears that surfaced? The act of confronting something we fear is liberating and empowering. I remember the first time I tried snorkeling. It may not seem like much, but after nearly drowning in my youth, I had

a terrible fear of water. I still vividly remember putting on the mask and snorkel and dipping my head into the water, only to quickly pull it out in a panic. But then I looked around at the lovely, serene sea, and I decided to give it one more try. I did, and today I count snorkeling and diving among my favorite pastimes.

Today I will attempt something I have avoided in the past. Perhaps I will apply for that dream job or sign up for a class that will bring me one step closer to it.

The Definition of Success

"There is only one success—to be able to spend your own life in your own way."
Christopher Morley

When you think of the word *success*, what comes to mind? Wealth? Fame? A Nobel Prize? Realistically, only a small percentage of us will ever actually achieve such narrow definitions of success. Allow yourself to sincerely believe that each and every one of us *can* experience success in this life—it all depends on how you define it. And one of the surest paths to success is to figure out what your purpose is and go after it. Not as easy as it sounds, sure; but just acknowledging and beginning the process will make you more successful today than you were yesterday!

Today I will write down one thing I can realistically accomplish that will make me feel successful.

Be a Fortress

"Each of us is an impregnable fortress that can be laid waste only from within."

Timothy J. Flynn

*O*ften, we can be our own worst enemies. Many of us hold on to self-defeating thoughts or actions, and it can be terribly difficult to rid ourselves of these destructive habits. The good news is, if we take time to reflect every day, we can often pinpoint moments when we allowed ourselves to fall victim to these silly tendencies. Once we identify our vulnerable

moments, we can begin the work of fighting these behaviors and starting better habits. Ready to be transformed, we are willing to examine these tendencies honestly and look for new positive thoughts and actions that can take their place.

Today I will review my day and analyze any self-defeating thought, behavior, or habit and take the first step in overcoming it.

Forever Young

"Age is not measured by years. Nature does not equally distribute energy. Some people are born old and tired while others are going strong at seventy."
Dorothy Thompson

*A*ge is something of a lifestyle choice. I am always inspired when I see or read about someone older than I am doing something I would only dream of doing now. There are folks in their 60s, 70s, 80s, and beyond who are getting degrees, waterskiing, and parachuting out of airplanes! I'd like to think I still have a chance to be like them when I "grow up."

Today I will take an assessment of my true age—am I a youngin' or an old fogey at heart? If I don't like the answer, I will push myself to grow younger at heart.

Claim Your Power

"The most common way people give up their power is by thinking they don't have any."

Alice Walker

Everyone has power. Some power is more obvious than others, but we all have some, nonetheless. Power is the ability to do something—to do anything! It can be easy to feel overwhelmed and powerless by the magnitude of the issues that surround us, but we can all choose to be proactive instead of just sitting back and worrying and complaining. We can't solve every problem, but we can do our part. When you look around you, what bothers you most? If you are most concerned about the homeless, donate money or supplies to a local shelter. If you worry about kids dropping out of school, volunteer to be a tutor or a mentor. We all have the power to make some difference, and who knows what big changes might come out of "small" work. Our choices are our power!

Today I will summon my power and use it to achieve some good.

111

There's No Avoiding Blisters

"In life as in the dance,
grace glides on blistered feet."
Alice Abrams

*D*ance often appears graceful and effortless, but the dancers themselves know the real story: quivering muscles, sweaty skin, labored breathing—and bruised, calloused feet. The dancers beam through it all, focused on their part in a beautiful whole. It truly is the same with life; we all have our troubles and travails, but we fight through the harder moments in preparation for a share in the more glorious ones.

Today I will put any aches, pains, or troubles out of my mind and focus on my dreams.

Tough Questions

"I don't think a tough question is disrespectful."
Helen Thomas

*H*ave you ever been in a situation where a leader was asked a question he or she obviously didn't want to be asked? Maybe it challenged them, or took the discussion in a different direction than they wanted. Or maybe they just didn't know the answer! In any case, a question—even a difficult or unwelcome one—is rarely actually inappropriate. Perhaps it misses the point, but in that case, it is only a misunderstanding that can be cleared up quickly. Questions promote discussion, and discussion is merely communication—and communication is often how things get done!

Today I will not hesitate to ask a question, and if a question is asked of me, I will think carefully and answer it as best I can.

Jump Right In

*"Life shrinks and expands
according to one's courage."*

Anaïs Nin

*H*ow scary new things can be! Going
off to school, interviewing for a job,
asking someone on a
date, traveling to an
unknown place... I still
get butterflies thinking of
some of these experiences
in my own past—and now
I know joy and exultation
because I faced them.
When we get comfortable,

life can get boring and tedious, but when we take on new challenges—especially a new "first"— we feel expansive and alive. Boldness really does have magic in it!

If I am faced with something that makes me a little nervous today, I will be bold and jump right in.

Puzzle Pieces

"One of the signs of passing youth is the birth of a sense of fellowship with other human beings as we take our place among them."

Virginia Woolf

When I was younger, my every thought was about me, me, me. I thought the universe revolved around me. As I have grown and taken on different jobs, friendships, and experiences, however, I have come to marvel at the many things I have in common with other people. I see how beautiful it is when we can work together and accomplish something great by putting the strengths and talents of

every one of us to use. Each of us is truly one piece in this beautiful, magnificent puzzle of life.

Today I will shift my focus to those around me. I will notice the unique strengths of others, and I will acknowledge them.

Simplicity Is Happiness

*"One is happy as a result of one's own efforts,
once one knows the necessary ingredients of
happiness—simple tastes, a certain degree of
courage, self denial to a point, love of work,
and, above all, a clear conscience. Happiness is
no vague dream, of that I now feel certain."*

George Sand

When I was a teenager, I dreamed about the day I would grow up and be a famous movie star living in a huge mansion. Now I am wiser, and I realize that happiness is found in the simple things: a gorgeous sunrise, fulfilling work, precious time with loved ones. When I focus on these beautiful aspects of my daily life, I cannot help but walk around with a broad smile on my face.

Today I will not let one single piece of beauty in my life drift by without being noticed.

Keep Your Chin Up

*"The greatest test of courage on earth is
to bear defeat without losing heart."*
Robert Green Ingersoll

One of life's hard truths is that it will
sometimes seem as though there are
challenges around every
corner. It can happen when
you are trying to further
your education. It can enter
after the honeymoon phase
of marriage. It can hit you
during your later years, even
though you had expected a
time of ease, comfort, and
relaxation. Just as most of
us will experience times of
peace and happiness, most
of us will also experience
times of difficulty, defeat, and

heartache. If we can see these times as proving grounds for later successes, we can keep our chins up. Each day truly is a new day (and each hour is a new hour, in fact!); who knows what great things are in store for us?

If I hit a wall today, I will do something to strengthen my heart: listen to good music, read an uplifting poem or book, or meet with a reassuring friend at a favorite park.

Lucky in Loss

"I hold it true, whate'er befall; I feel it when I sorrow most; 'Tis better to have loved and lost; Than never to have loved at all."

Alfred, Lord Tennyson

A couple of years ago, when we buried two pets in one month, it was hard for my children to wrap their heads around the above sentiment. I tried to explain as best I could that while we were sad and our grief was hard to bear, we were lucky to have had such tender, loving creatures in our lives for so long. Grief is a painful process, but it has

a silver lining. Those who've experienced loss tend to say "I love you" more often—and more sincerely. They laugh more easily, appreciate the little things, and are less likely to take others for granted. They have learned the lesson that life is fragile and love is precious.

Today I will be mindful of the fleeting nature of life, and I will love without holding back.

So Close

"The line between failure and success is so fine that we scarcely know when we pass it—so fine that we often are on the line and do not know it."
Ralph Waldo Emerson

When we look back on some of our accomplishments, they can strike us as funny. It is such a relief to have them done. In hindsight things seem so clear, but while you're in the midst of your work, the end can sometimes seem so elusive; it can be easy to get discouraged. Once we've achieved our goal we can look back at our unknowing selves and say, "I can't believe I almost gave up at that point, when I was so close!" Keep going—you *are* getting there!

Today I will keep going no matter what. I will not give in to discouragement.

Push Through

"Life is not easy for any of us. But what of that? We must have perseverance and above all confidence in ourselves. We must believe that we are gifted for something and that this thing must be attained."

Marie Curie

When you are faced with a roadblock in life, how do you react? Are you deflated, or does it spark your mind to come up with a solution to the problem at hand? Feeling deflated is the easy response, but we owe it to ourselves to summon our confidence and push through. No matter who we are, at some point in our lives we have tasted success, whether we are a whiz with numbers or excel at athletics or have the compassion it takes to go into the social-work or medical fields. While we are

not all as smart or talented as Albert Einstein or Toni Morrison, we all have talents and gifts we can strengthen and hone.

Today I will push through any difficult circumstance by putting my unique gifts and talents to creative use.

How About Now?

*M*any of us fall into the trap of putting things off. We'd like to have a job that pays better, presents more challenge, or offers more creativity, but we leave off doing much about it. We want to get fit and healthy, but we figure we'll "start tomorrow." We yearn for more companionship with others, but we wait for others to invite us over or make plans. Get something started right now. Make the first move toward your most desired goal.

Today, if I find myself daydreaming about a goal or desire, I will figure out a way to make it happen.

Tending to My Sphere

"Every person is responsible for all the good within the scope of his abilities, and for no more, and none can tell whose sphere is the largest."

Gail Hamilton

*A*ll the needs in the world can seem overwhelming. The world is not fair; we all learn that hard concept at a young age. We can choose to be depressed by that, or we can take it as a challenge. We all can make a difference, and many small differences add up to big change. Don't attempt to take on the world's problems by yourself—just

focus on your part. Vote in every election—or run for office yourself if you think it's a good fit for you. Seize a need in your own sphere and focus on that. This way you will be one of the lucky ones who, in old age, can look back over a lifetime of achievements.

Today I will seize an opportunity to change my world for the better.

Sharpen Your Saw

"Work is the greatest thing in the world, so we should always save some of it for tomorrow."
Don Herold

Have you ever run yourself ragged, trying to finish everything in one day? Certainly at times this is necessary, but some of us get in such a habit of accomplishing as much as possible every single day, we forget to just slow down once in a while.

As essential as work is, everyone needs some downtime. Working through lunch every day and putting off vacations time and time again only hurts us in the end. Once in a while, leave something unfinished and take a refresher. "Sharpening the saw" is one name for this breather, and such breaks have been proven to actually improve productivity once we return to our task with renewed purpose and vigor.

Feeling up to the challenges each new day brings doesn't just happen. We have to consciously *do* things that will re-invigorate us—things that nourish our body, mind, heart, and soul. For you this might mean taking time for a leisurely lunch with a dear friend, a five-mile bike ride, a yoga class, or an evening with a good book.

This evening I will sharpen my saw, so that tomorrow I will cut through my work faster and more efficiently.

Be Who You Are

*"Let us then be what we are,
and speak what we think."*

Henry Wadsworth Longfellow

any of us try to emulate another person—often someone we see as prettier, smarter, or funnier than we are. Or we fall into the trap of not speaking up because we are afraid of what others will think. If everyone tried to be like everyone else or if everyone stayed silent because they were afraid of being criticized, our society would lose its flavor and vibrancy. Our differences keep things interesting, and they stimulate growth. So

speak up—and be yourself. True, you may end up regretting a comment, but this happens to everyone at one time or another. This is how we grow and learn—by reflecting on issues and talking about them.

Today I will be proud of who I am, and I will not hesitate to get a lively conversation started.

Bring It On

"I have reached a point in my life where I understand the pain and the challenges; and my attitude is one of standing up with open arms to meet them all."

Myrlie Evers

When I was young, I had little use for the stories my elders would tell me of how they overcame challenges and suffering. But now I realize they were trying to teach me a powerful and valuable lesson—that challenges and suffering are the things that mold us into our beautiful, complete selves.

Today I will meet all challenges head-on.

Live a Little

"Life is either a tight-rope or a feather bed. Give me the tight-rope."

Edith Wharton

$\mathcal{M}$ost of us are much more talented and capable than we realize. Often the component missing in our lives that would allow us to access these capabilities is risk. *Risk*—the very word can make us shudder. On the other hand, a life without risk can be safe and dreary to the point of being a life wasted. On your deathbed, are you going to be grateful that you led a predictable life? Or will you wish that you'd had the courage to take risks and chase your dreams?

Today I will cast aside my doubts and self-imposed limitations. I will be game to get out there and live my life.

Elusive Wisdom

"Knowledge can be communicated,
but not wisdom. One can find it, live it,
be fortified by it, do wonders through it,
but one cannot communicate and teach it."
Herman Hesse

Wisdom comes
from life
experience and making
connections between
different events.
Everyone's experiences
are somewhat
different; you can at
times share bits of
wisdom, but if the
other person is not at
a point in their life to
understand it, it will
not "take." Knowing
varied bits of wisdom
does not make you
an all-around wise

person, anyway. Many people are wise, but they are wise in their own unique ways and with their own specific outlooks. It is easy to mistake knowledge for wisdom, and vice versa. Some people find it helpful to think of wisdom as something you learn with your heart instead of your brain. It is "heart knowledge."

Today I will try to soak in as much wisdom as I can. I will let my heart be my guide.

Treasured Chores

*"I do some of my best thinking
while pulling weeds."*
Martha Smith

Have you ever had the experience of doing a simple chore such as cleaning the bathroom and suddenly realized how clear your thinking had become? Many people find cleaning and other basic chores renewing. Perhaps the feeling is due to our innate pleasure and gratitude for having such beautiful or helpful things in our lives; we instinctively desire to take good care of them. Or perhaps the feeling is merely the result of focusing on something simple for a time without any distractions. In any case, these basic activities have a way of clearing the cobwebs and recharging creative batteries

surprisingly well. So when it's time to clean the bathroom or prune the bushes, settle in with your tools and renew your mind as you renew your living space!

Today I will enjoy my chores and the renewed focus and order that they bring to my life.

Creativity Is Calling

"Wise men say it isn't art! But what of it, if it is children and love in paint?"
Georgia O'Keeffe

⌐

Art used to seem so limited to an "elite" crowd. I'm sure this atmosphere stifled many a budding artist's creativity. Not so anymore. The Internet and other new outlets have opened up the world of expression to the masses, with delightful results. If you have ever had negative feedback about how you paint, write, dance, or draw (even if you yourself were doing the judging), shake it off and begin anew. Don't keep your inner masterpiece all to yourself!

Today I will create something. Maybe instead of purchasing a trendy necklace, I will try my hand at making one instead.

Generating Happiness

"To be happy, you must learn to forget yourself."
Edward Bulwer-Lytton

recently read an article about how people today are more narcissistic than in past generations. No wonder so many of us are unhappy and feel purposeless! True, deep happiness is found when we set our sights outward. We step outside of our own realm and discover new places, experiences, ideas, and companions. Before we know it, we are positively submerged in happiness!

I will find ways throughout my day to focus on things that go beyond my own existence.

Sunny Skies Up Ahead

"Don't let one cloud obliterate the whole sky."
Anaïs Nin

Have you ever made a problem bigger than it needed to be? Most of us have done it: zoom in on one bad word, action, or issue and let it ruin our whole day (or week!). When we sense our feelings spiraling downward in this way, we need to simply step back and refocus. Think of the last thing that made you happy—maybe a witty joke or a delicious meal with loved ones. Bask in that past event for a moment, then begin anew today.

If something upsetting happens today, I will take a moment to refocus and renew my spirit.

Collaboration Works Magic

"Light is the task where many share the toil."

Homer

‎

Certain jobs can seem insurmountable unless you tap into a little teamwork. When you do, it is amazing how quickly things can get done! Think of the cleanup involved after a Thanksgiving feast, for instance. For one person, it could take hours, but if many pitch in and help—and enjoy some good conversation—the whole job could be over in less than an hour. Teamwork works!

If someone close to me seems intimidated by a large task today, I will figure out a way to pitch in and help.

153

Don't Just Sit There

"If I were to suggest a general rule for happiness, I would say work a little harder; work a little longer; work!"

Frederick H. Ecker

———

Among the most gratifying feelings in life is the feeling of being useful. This may seem contrary to modern advertising messages and other elements in today's culture, but it is a timeless truth. Everyone wants to feel needed, from the youngest children to the oldest citizens. Once babies are capable of much movement at all, they are not content just sitting there for very long. And if elderly people are at a point in their lives where it is difficult to get around, they still want to be active any way they can, from communicating with loved ones to keeping up to date on world events. Even those of us who pine for idle vacations often find that when our wish is granted, we feel unfulfilled and disappointed. So be active until it is time to retire for the evening. You will soon find yourself feeling fulfilled and exuberant.

Today I will work hard at every task and take pride in my finished projects.

Tough Decisions

*"A mistake in judgment isn't fatal, but
too much anxiety about judgment is."*

Pauline Kael

*H*ave you ever gotten on your own nerves by hemming and hawing about what course of action to take in a given situation? Just think carefully, make your choice, and go with it. There are many difficult decisions to be made in life, from college or career choices to whether or not to pursue a certain relationship to where to settle down—the list is endless. Analyze the options and get started. Delaying things is evidence of insecurity and immaturity, and you are too strong to fall into such traps. If in the future you regret a certain choice, you can always change course or make amends.

Today I will make any tough decisions as quickly as possible, and I will move on.

Perfecting the System

"We too often bind ourselves by authorities rather than by the truth."

Lucretia Mott

here is never a shortage of people in the world ready to tell us how to live our lives and what we should believe. From authority figures like politicians and church leaders to parents, teachers, and doctors, advice (good and bad) is always coming at us from every direction. But sometimes the best advice comes from within, our inner voice that is sometimes hard to hear above those louder, exterior

voices. Whenever we start to feel a little constrained, we should think carefully. Are we held back by reasonable guidelines or because no one has bothered to try to come up with a better way of doing things?

Today I will listen to my own inner voice, determine my own opinion, and speak my own truth.

Life Is Good

"Courage, it would seem, is nothing less than the power to overcome danger, misfortune, fear, injustice, while continuing to affirm inwardly that life with all its sorrows is good."
Dorothy Thompson

⎯⎯⎯⎯⎯

The bravest people are not those who never feared. In fact, those who had to lead in battle, fight rampant injustice, or stand up to horrible crimes likely felt more than a twinge of fear during their clashes. They did not give in to the fear and let it stop them, though. They summoned something greater than the fear: their own courage. Courage comes from a deep belief about how life can and should be—and how good it is. The mere fact that they took action proves this, for why would someone bother taking action unless he or she thought the desired change would last and be worth the work and risk involved?

Today, I will approach any objectionable situation with courage, even if—deep down—I am a little scared.

Case Open

"I do not think that I will ever reach a stage when I will say, 'This is what I believe. Finished.' What I believe is alive... and open to growth."
Madeleine L'Engle

If we say, "Case closed on life—I have nothing more to learn," what do we do then? Such an attitude is amazingly closed-minded (though not final, as any mind can be opened at any time). It is good to always be open to new experiences and to growth. Even taking a walk over to the next block might have us encountering something we have never seen before and know nothing about—perhaps a tantalizing new dish at a local restaurant, an amazing flower in full bloom, or an unfamiliar play. Branch out and grow. Something spectacular might be right around the corner.

Today, I will branch out, whether for something small like visiting a museum I haven't been to in a while or something big like booking a trip to a distant land.

Govern Yourself First

"Self government is no less essential to the development, growth and happiness of the individual than to the nation."

William H. Douglas

*N*ations need strong, judicious governments to be the best collectives they can be. As individuals, we also need to be strong and judicious to run our own lives and affairs in the best possible way. If we are not in control and do not govern ourselves properly, our lives can easily run off track. Strong and happy people make a strong and happy nation!

Today I will make a list of three ways I can govern my own life better, and I will get started.

Let Go and Let Love In

"The more anger towards the past you carry in your heart, the less capable you are of loving in the present."

Barbara De Angelis

———

I recently came across the story of Corrie ten Boom, who was imprisoned in the Ravensbrück concentration camp during World War II for helping Jews. Years after the war, she saw one of her former prison guards after she had given a presentation about her wartime experiences. The guard, who had been one of the most sadistic of the guards ten Boom had encountered, came up after the presentation to commend ten Boom on her talk. He told her that he had been a guard at Ravensbrück (he did not remember ten Boom, but she surely remembered him). He told her that since the war, he had come to the realization of the horrors of his actions and had dedicated his life to making amends in any way that he could. He stretched out his hand and asked ten Boom if she would make peace with him. Ten Boom struggled with the confusion and hate mixed up inside her.

I can lift my hand, she thought. *I can do that much.* Corrie later wrote of the experience: "For a long moment we grasped each other's hands, the former guard and the former prisoner." She was surprised by the peace she felt at the center of her being at that moment.

Today I will forgive someone who has wronged me—as much for my own peace as for theirs.

A Welcoming Garden

"Gardens and flowers have a way of bringing people together, drawing them from their homes."
Clare Ansberry

The tradition of gardens and front porches is almost lost in today's society. It is as though we want our homes to appear nice and ordered, but we stop short of making them appear welcoming. I sigh with longing whenever I come across a pretty, flowery front garden. So, this spring I am going to do it: I will plant an arrangement of blooming plants and add pots and a hanging basket to my porch. My front yard will be beautiful—and welcoming. Perhaps it will be a conversation starter with a new neighbor, and my block will seem a little more friendly because of it.

Today I will beautify my home in a way that others will see, and if I come across someone else's beautiful front yard, I will start a conversation about it.

Having It All

"What helps luck is a habit of watching for opportunities, of having a patient, but restless mind, of sacrificing one's ease or vanity, of uniting a love of detail to foresight, and of passing through hard times bravely and cheerfully."

Charles Victor Cherbuliez

When I was younger, I used to envy people who seemed to "have all the luck." As I've grown wiser, though, I do believe the above quote rings true. People are lucky in different ways. If most of us stop to think about it, we have elements in our lives that would make others envious. "Having it all" stems from feeling at peace deep inside. This peaceful center helps us to handle hard times bravely and with good cheer, and it helps us to keep a quiet but watchful mind. Lucky people tend to be very deliberate, patient, and mindful of important details as well as their main object.

Today I will maintain my peaceful center at all times; I will not let any opportunity pass me by.

All Are Welcome

"If we are to achieve a richer culture, rich in contrasting values, we must recognize the whole gamut of human potentialities, and so weave a less arbitrary social fabric, one in which each diverse human gift will find a fitting place."

Margaret Mead

Sometimes it seems that certain people are more welcome and involved in society than others are. Why is that? Sometimes it has to do with finances and ethnicity, other times with perceived abilities and intelligence, and still other times with health and wellness. Everyone has something to offer, though, from the obviously talented athlete or scientist to the artistic individual who happens to have a disability to the caring, nurturing individual who has fallen on hard times financially. Every individual we come across is different from us in many ways but similar to us in others. It is the differences that add vibrancy and interest to life.

Today I will pay attention during my interactions with those around me. I will try to pinpoint the talents and capabilities of others, and I will help and encourage them to succeed in any way I can.

Our Own Parts

"We do not choose our own parts in life...
Our duty is confined to playing them well."
Epictetus

A popular saying of my grandfather's was, "We have to play the hand we were dealt." It took me a long time to understand that this saying simply meant that our job is to take what life gave us and do the best we can with it. We don't choose our family, our nationality, or even our gender, but we can use our unique set of circumstances as a jumping-off point for an amazing life story!

Today I will make good choices and make the most of my circumstances, talents, and opportunities.

Imagine the Possibilities

"Great necessities call out great virtues."
Abigail Adams

───⌁───

When we are faced with times of great difficulty, it becomes necessary to get creative and make the circumstances and resources at hand work for our needs. Often at such times we are surprised by our own resourcefulness and capabilities. If only we could summon such greatness at other times as well!

Today I will pretend that all of my efforts are toward a great necessity. Perhaps even I will be dazzled by my accomplishments!

This Moment Affects the Future

"The present was an egg laid by the past that had the future inside its shell."

Zora Neale Hurston

What I did in the past affects me today, just like everything I do today will affect my future. Sometimes I look back on my actions and grimace with regret, and other times I look back and smile with pride. I am happier when I am proud of my choices.

Today I will make good choices, aware that my future depends on it. I will not let my future self down!

Reach for the Stars

"Far away there in the sunshine are my highest aspirations. I may not reach them, but I can look up and see their beauty, believe in them, and try to follow where they lead."

Louisa May Alcott

*D*aily life is so full of duties and commitments that my dreams often take a backseat to my to-do list and to the demands of work and loved ones. Some nights I consider myself lucky if I have time to read a single page of a book at night before I fall asleep, exhausted! But I know my dreams are always there on the periphery, waiting for me to make a move toward them. I need to make them more of a priority in my life.

Today I will reflect on what my highest aspirations are, and I will take one definite step toward one of them.

Praise and Criticism

"As a solid rock is not shaken by a strong gale, so wise persons remain unaffected by praise or censure."

Siddhartha Gautama

———

While it is easy to let praise go to our heads, it also takes a mature nature to handle criticism well. The trick is to take both with equanimity. If someone praises you, of course say "thank you" (and perhaps beam inside!), but don't allow yourself to become complacent or prideful. There are always new challenges that lead to more growth. On the other hand, if you work really hard on something and receive criticism on it, analyze the criticism. Is there truth in any of the criticism? Be honest! Work can always be improved. After you have reflected, make the changes you agree with and move on to the next task.

Today I resolve to receive praise with equanimity and criticism with thoughtful reflection.

Free Therapy

*"Surely there is something in the unruffled
calm of nature that overawes our little
anxieties and doubts: the sight of the deep-
blue sky, and the clustering stars above,
seem to impart a quiet to the mind."*

Jonathan Edwards

I grew up in a house with woods and a lake behind it, and as a child, I was always outside, close to nature. I would play and explore endlessly; it was so calm and peaceful, at times it was almost like a meditation session.

Today when I go for walks along nature paths, I again feel that blissful serenity. Nature is free therapy—the best kind of self-help available!

No matter how busy I get today, I will take ten minutes to go outside and gather my thoughts.

The Measure of Success

"I can honestly say that I was never affected by the question of the success of an undertaking. If I felt it was the right thing to do, I was for it regardless of the possible outcome."

Golda Meir

Have you ever had the urge to take something up but then didn't because you weren't sure it could succeed? Many people give in to such doubts. It is important, though, to really reflect about what course of action will make you happier. Perhaps your favorite thing to do is cook; you dream of opening your own restaurant, but your current job is in accounting. Should you take the leap? Do your research and set up a plan—and follow your heart. Perhaps a small step toward your dream would be to start culinary school part-time or apply to work some hours cooking at a restaurant you love. See how that goes, and follow where your heart leads.

Today I vow to do the right thing without hesitation.

Live in Love

"Love lights more fires than hate extinguishes."
Ella Wheeler Wilcox

When we are hurt, it can be tempting to lash out. What often happens, though, is that we waste a lot of time and energy on stewing and ugliness when we could be happy and channeling love. Sound impossible? When did revenge and anger ever make anyone truly happy? I know in my experience, it may have felt gratifying in the moment, but I usually looked back on my feelings and actions with regret. It is much better and more beautiful to respond with love or—if that is impossible—turn our attentions somewhere else, so we can regain loving feelings.

If someone hurts me or I feel anger simmering inside me today, I will respond with love or make an effort to move on from my negative feelings toward love.

Dreaming Sets the
Stage for Doing

*"It is in our idleness, in our dreams, that the
submerged truth sometimes comes to the top."*

Virginia Woolf

*H*ow guilty I sometimes feel when I take a day off from work! But it is often during those brief blocks of rest that I am pleasantly surprised by great ideas and insights that seem to magically come to me. Reflection breeds innovation!

Today I will set ten minutes aside to daydream, let my mind wander, and reflect.

Positive Ripples

"You cannot hope to build a better world without improving the individuals. To that end, each of us must work for his own improvement, and at the same time share a general responsibility for all humanity, our particular duty being to aid those to whom we think we can be most useful."

Marie Curie

*M*any of us complain about our governments and events around the world without always thinking about what our role could be in making things better. It can be intimidating, but I know I can start by improving myself first, then looking around for something close at hand that I am capable of helping out with. Like pebbles thrown into a pond, my deeds will form positive ripples that move outward to distant shores.

Today I will begin to reform a bad habit or start a good one, and tomorrow I will pick something in my community to work on.

Enlivening Communication

"Good communication is as stimulating as black coffee, and just as hard to sleep after."
Anne Morrow Lindbergh

*M*any of us have had the experience in which a seemingly casual question has

led to a deep, meaningful discussion. In these moments we feel alive and productive and sense a deep kinship with others. Discuss! Communicate! It is how most things get done.

Today I will be open to communication with those around me. I will voice my opinion and be respectful of the opinions of others.

Looking Forward

"The great use of life is to spend it for something that will outlast it."
William James

When you examine your daily life, what evidence of the past do you see? We have automobiles, and the inventors of those are long gone. Even the wise quotes in this book are evidence of writers and important figures from history. In the same way, we can each contribute to something that will live on, whether by volunteering for a venerable organization or being the best parent or teacher you can be so your children or pupils can one day change the world for the better. Focus on beautiful, lasting details rather than passing trends that change every other week.

Today I will spend time doing something that will outlast me. Perhaps I will tutor or coach a child, plant a tree, or get more involved in local recycling efforts.

First, Be Brave

*"Courage is the ladder on which
all other virtues mount."*
Clare Boothe Luce

⟜⟞

*N*one of us can fully cultivate any of the other virtues before we first have the courage to really examine our lives truthfully and figure out what areas need improvement. It takes courage to be this honest and true to ourselves. The easier route would be to just carry on and do as we please in any moment without much regard to the bigger picture. Courage leads us on a unique path.

Today I will be brave. It will not be easy, but I will always choose to take the bold step that needs to be taken.

Work That Wows

"To fulfill a dream, to be allowed to sweat over lonely labor, to be given a chance to create, is the meat and potatoes of life. The money is the gravy. As everyone else, I love to dunk my crust in it. But alone, it is not a diet designed to keep body and soul together."

Bette Davis

Long ago, my grandfather worked as a bricklayer. Fireplaces and garden walls were his favorite projects. He took pride in his work and was able to make a good living. That is happiness—to thrive doing work you love to do. Pride in their work is what makes people eagerly get out of bed each day.

Today I will make sure to spend some time on work that I love, whether it's paid work or a hobby such as gardening or blogging.

My Own Work in Progress

"We cannot have a world where everyone is a victim. 'I'm this way because my father made me this way. I'm this way because my husband made me this way.' Yes, we are indeed formed by traumas that happened to us. But you must take charge, you must take over, you are responsible."

Camille Paglia

When we pay close attention, we can see evidence of people blaming others for the state of their lives every day. I have to admit, I indulge in this behavior myself from time to time. Sometimes when I get stressed out, my anger gets the best of me. It is easy to reflect and think, *I got my temper from my dad.* At this point in my life, though, I must have chosen that temper for myself, for I am not a little girl anymore. I have read plenty of self-help articles about taking time for yoga and other relaxation techniques; I need to start putting those techniques into practice. I am still a work in progress, but I am my own work in progress—no one else's.

Today I am in charge, and my choices will be good ones.

Wisdom Through Writing

*"To write is to descend, to excavate,
to go underground."*

Anaïs Nin

Most of us spend some time writing, whether we write for a living, for business purposes, or to communicate with loved ones. It is easy to take writing for granted, especially in this era of e-mails and social media posts, but it is truly a wonderful tool. Most of us—as we write—go back over our words, measuring them and making sure we are conveying exactly what we want to say. One small word that is not quite right can throw off an entire piece of communication. When we write, we really think about our subject, and we often learn as much from the exercise as we convey to the other person.

Tonight I will journal about my day so that none of its meaning will be lost to me.

Soft Summer Breezes

"What is more gentle than a wind in summer?"
John Keats

*E*very season has its treasured moments,
from the freshness of spring to the

warmth of summer to the crispness of fall to
the still beauty of winter. I try to set aside
blocks of time during each season to just be
outside, taking it all in. These moments never
fail to freshen my mind and renew my spirit.

**Today I will dedicate 20 minutes to marvel at
the beauty of nature.**

Speak, Write, or Paint

"I found I could say things with colors that I couldn't say in any other way— things I had no words for."

Georgia O'Keeffe

*E*ach of us has a preferred style of communication and of expressing ourselves. For some it is speaking, for others it is writing, and for still others it is through drawing or painting. Figure out what your style is, embrace it, and use it!

I will focus on honing my communication skills today, and I will get my point across.

Where Happiness Belongs

"It is not easy to find happiness in ourselves,
and it is not possible to find it elsewhere."
Agnes Repplier

appiness is complex. It seems so
simple, but in our busy modern
world full of possessions,
appointments, and events,
it is easy to search and
search and wind up feeling
empty in the midst of so
much activity and among
so many things. The trick,
I believe, is to cultivate and
tap into a store of happiness
at the core of our being.
Nothing else can fill up that
place inside us where the
happiness belongs. You can
try finding love and making
that your core, but it won't
fill up that place. You can
try making the most money
humanly possible, but

again—it will not fill up that place. You can try food or drink, but you will only feel emptier still. Analyze yourself and pinpoint what makes you unique, then treasure those qualities and make the most of them. Call them to mind when you find yourself feeling uncertain in this world.

Today I will contemplate my strengths, and I will put them to use and be happy.

The Blame Game Is No Fun

*"Take a look at those two open hands
of yours. They are tools with which to
serve, make friends, and reach out for the
best in life. Open hands open the way to
achievement. Put them to work today."*
Wilferd A. Peterson

***

*L*isten to the news on the radio or watch
it on TV, and it's very common to
witness people playing the blame game. I don't
want to take part in that game. I know that
my community is far from perfect, and we
all share some of the blame for it. We all are
responsible for certain aspects of our lives and
our world, and if we fall down on any aspect
of the job, it affects the whole. It is in *our*
hands to make things better.

**Today I will survey my own corner of my
world and tend to any areas that need work.**

Ageless

"A woman has the age she deserves."
Coco Chanel

I have known people in their 70s who seemed much younger, and I have also observed the reverse—women in their 20s who could almost have passed for 40. Some of it,

no doubt, has to do with genes, exercise, and nutrition, but some of it surely has to do with attitude as well. If you dread your alarm going off and plod into work each day, you will seem old and tired, while if you are excited by the possibilities each new day holds and greet it with a smile, you can seem far younger than your years.

Today I will be happy and smile, and it will take years off my face.

Knock, Knock. Who's There?

"Not many sounds in life, and I include all urban and rural sounds, exceed in interest a knock at the door."

Charles Lamb

Curiosity is a marvelous thing. A knock at the door, like birthdays and sunrises, holds mystery, promise, and possibility. Is it a dear friend stopping by for a chat? The mail carrier delivering that item we ordered? A neighbor with a question? It could just as easily be a solicitor or other unwelcome intrusion, of course. But even those less-desired visits, when looked at in the right light, can

be invitations to serve someone or make a new acquaintance. You might be the one person all day who smiled and was kind to someone with an unpleasant job.

Today I will welcome each interruption— phone call, knock on the door, or otherwise—as an opportunity to chat.

Soul Food

Travel is transforming. Although often it's our differences from others in distant lands that are most apparent, travel opens our eyes to our similarities as well. The reality is that most people in the world want the same things we do— happiness, peace, a better life, a better future for their children. Traveling not only teaches you about others, it teaches you important lessons about yourself and your own culture. Often you get an entirely new perspective from the outside looking back in.

Today I will start planning my next journey, whether across the ocean or across the state.

Disconnect Now and Then

"I love people. I love my family, my children…but inside myself is a place where I live all alone and that's where you renew your springs that never dry up."

Pearl S. Buck

With today's cell phones, e-mail, and social media sites, I feel like I am always interacting with somebody. It's great to be able to connect with loved ones so quickly, but sometimes I still feel the need to just disconnect and be all by myself. Enjoying these quiet times now and then helps me stay in tune with myself, which is just as important (if not more so) as being in touch with others.

If I let weeks go by without indulging in a little "me time," I definitely see how it starts to affect my mood and relationships. I start to feel a little on edge, and I worry about not getting to do the things that I love and that I consider important. Downtime by myself helps me refocus and get my priorities back in order.

Today I will devote one hour to myself, whether that means waking up early, taking my lunch hour all to myself, or staying up one hour later. I will take some deep breaths, get centered, and enjoy the downtime.

Be Involved

"The good we secure for ourselves is precarious and uncertain until it is secured for all of us and incorporated into our common life."

Jane Addams

Accomplishing things and reaping rewards are good things. We all wish for that promotion, or that new car, or even to win the lottery! But it is not good to keep all the winnings of life to ourselves, for what good does it ultimately do if we jealously hoard it all in the end? Indeed, we can't take it with us! On the other hand, share your good fortune, and you lift everyone up with you, whether you have a wealth of happiness or a financial boon.

Today I will share my good fortune, even in a small gift of a smile to a stranger or a one-dollar donation to charity.

This Moment Right Now

"Remember, remember, this is now, and now, and now. Live it, feel it, cling to it."

Sylvia Plath

The one thing many of us wish we had more of is time. Maybe it's because instead of focusing and savoring the present moment, we devote much of our time to regretting the past or worrying about the future. Before we know it, years have passed, and we feel like we have so many lost dreams. This is so unnecessary. The moment before us is precious, and we can make the most of it.

Right now I will focus on the present moment. If it was the last moment of my life, what would I most want to do with it? Today I will pursue my most-desired goal, no excuses.

Say Yes

"Small opportunities are often the beginning of great enterprises."
Demosthenes

Opportunities come to us every day, but often we do not recognize them. Last week I was invited to a party; I felt lazy that day and responded that I had a conflict and could not make it. It is okay to do that from time to time if you are feeling spent, but if you find yourself feeling a little down or feeling out of touch, go to every party you're invited to for a while. Throw some parties of your own, and invite a wide range of acquaintances. Who knows if a chance meeting will turn into a wonderful new relationship or a networking connection.

Today I will say yes to any invitation I receive, and I will start planning a future get-together at my home.

Anything Can Be Improved

"If you have nothing else to do, look about you and see if there isn't something close at hand that you can improve! It may make you wealthy, though it is more likely that it will make you happy."

George Matthew Adams

*S*ometimes I get so busy, I forget to notice how my surroundings are affecting me. Take my home, for instance— there are so many ways I could beautify it, clear out clutter, fix things up, and really improve my living space. This is where I spend most of my time. It should be beautiful and make me happy!

Today I will survey my home, make a list of things that need improvement, and get started on one of them.

Choose Cheerfulness

"Life's race can best be run with a light heart
and a buoyant countenance. Cheerfulness
will open a door when other keys fail."

B. C. Forbes

———❧———

Isn't it wonderful to be in the presence
of someone who is usually smiling, who
mentions the good in things before the bad,
and who speaks only nice words? Cheerful
people are magnetic, and cheerfulness is
contagious. Once you start surrounding
yourself with cheerfulness and choosing to be
cheerful yourself, you will often find others
around you choosing it too.

**Today I will smile a lot, and I will use only
positive words.**

Happiness Was Born a Twin

"I have been in Sorrow's kitchen and licked out all the pots. Then I have stood on the peaky mountain wrapped in rainbows, with a harp and a sword in my hands."

Zora Neale Hurston

The duality of life is a given. Sorrow and joy are more like twin sisters than strangers. Often one follows the other, and sometimes we experience both at once.

I remember the poignant sweet-sadness of sharing warmth and laughter with my siblings after my grandmother passed away. The late-night talks I had with her during her last weeks as she lay in her hospital bed were priceless, and the songs we sang together brought me peace and strength. Even in the midst of trial and grief, we can experience glimpses of love, hope, and happiness.

If I feel sad today, I will allow myself to—but only for a little while. Then I will do something to turn the day around. Perhaps I will go visit a friend, take myself out to lunch, or better yet, find someone who has more reason to be sad than I do and help them with my whole heart.

Stir Crazy

"Be lazy, go crazy."
Margaret Mead

⌒⌒

Many of us dream of a more relaxed life, but when we actually get several days in a row like that we get a little stir crazy,

don't we? Some relaxing downtime now and then soothes our body and comforts our soul, but when we sense it turning into a prolonged bout of laziness, we must nip it in the bud.

Today I will do a physical activity to nurture my body and a mental activity to stimulate my mind. Today will not be a lazy day for me!

Simplicity

"To simplify is very nearly the whole of the
higher artistic process; finding what conventions
of form and what detail one can do without—
and yet preserve the spirit of the whole."
Willa Cather

Though many of us give in to a tendency
to make things more complex and
messy than they need to be, simplicity is
good for us in nearly every area of our lives.
Simplicity in regard to diet keeps us healthy
and vibrant. Simplicity in our homes and at
our workplaces keeps us efficient, productive,
and calm. Simplicity in our relationships
upholds the peace and avoids hurt feelings.
Effective simplifying is an impressive skill that
allows us to reap a prized treasure: more time.

**Today I will be on the watch for activities
that take up a lot of my time, and I will try to
figure out ways to simplify them.**

Let It Flow

"I know I cannot paint a flower. I cannot paint the sun on the desert on a bright summer morning, but maybe in terms of paint color I can convey to you my experience of the flower or the experience that makes the flower of significance to me at that particular time."

Georgia O'Keeffe

Some of us long to pursue an artistic endeavor but fail to even begin because we fear we will never be able to complete a great work. What of that? Michelangelo's first painting was not breathtaking, but he continued to follow his inspiration and create. We should follow our desires as well. Art is all about personal expression, and we all have something valuable and unique to convey.

Today I will let my inner artist out, whether by taking a pottery class, starting a draft of a short story or play, or designing a pair of earrings.

Visualize a Great Tomorrow

"Five minutes, just before going to sleep, given to a bit of directed imagination regarding achievement possibilities of the morrow, will steadily and increasingly bear fruit, particularly if all ideas of difficulty, worry or fear are resolutely ruled out and replaced by those of accomplishment and smiling courage."

Frederick Pierce

*L*ately when I lay my head on the pillow at night, it is as though the curtain goes up on a horror flick: What if they give me a dreaded task at work tomorrow? What if my son fails his test? What if my dad has a nasty

fall? The "what ifs" go on and on, and I wake up with even more worries on my mind. Most certainly a better way would be to start a habit of positive planning, even if just for the last five minutes before I go to bed. Maybe then I can replace my silly worries with positive hopes for the coming dawn, and I can awaken renewed, refreshed, and ready to go!

Tonight I will take charge of my mind. I will devote five minutes to visualizing a great tomorrow.

Learn to Love Learning

"Learning is not to be attained by chance; it must be sought with ardor and attended to with diligence."

Abigail Adams

$\mathcal{L}$ooking back on my school years, I can see that I was a lazy student. I am lucky that in the years after my schooling was over, I read many things and went many places that opened my mind and piqued my curiosity. Now I learn something every day by chance, and I make a point to learn at least one thing more. There are opportunities to learn around every corner, but we need to be attentive, and we must also seek them out. We miss a lot when we engage in lazy or passive learning.

Today I will pick a topic that interests me, and I will delve into it. Maybe I will do intensive research for an upcoming trip or I will visit a nearby museum and learn as much about one interesting topic as possible.

A Settled Purpose

"I have brought myself by long meditation to the conviction that a human being with a settled purpose must accomplish it, and that nothing can resist a will which will stake even existence upon its fulfillment."

Benjamin Disraeli

Can you think of something in your life for which you will "stake even existence"? This seems a bit heavy, but when most of us reflect on our lives, we realize that there are causes and people that are certainly worth this much to us. It is this type of reflection that can lead us to our true purpose in life. Do you wish for world peace? Maybe you could take a step toward peace in your community, perhaps by researching the biggest issues and volunteering in some way. Do you wish for better employment opportunities for the working poor? You could volunteer at a job center or donate some time to teaching adults English as a second language. All of us pushing and working, each in our own way, will make the world a better place for everyone.

Today I will take time to contemplate my purpose and figure out a way to express it in my daily life.

Art and Thought

"What do we have from the past?
Art and thought. That's what lasts.
That's what continues to feed people
and give them an idea of something better."
Susan Sontag

Art and thought do inspire us. If we go to a museum, we will be inspired by works both ancient and modern. In fact, some of the most insightful philosophy is from as long ago as ancient China, and scientists have found primitive works of art that are believed to date as far back as 43,000 years ago. Humans have always felt a longing to express themselves, get inspired, and communicate with others in creative ways. Art and thought lead to growth and innovative change.

Today I will create something new. Perhaps I will write a poem or begin work on a painting.

Nourishment from the World Around Us

"The final lesson a writer learns is that everything can nourish the writer. The dictionary, a new word, a voyage, an encounter, a talk on the street, a book, a phrase learned."

Anaïs Nin

*J*ust like any author, we are all "writers" of our own stories—our own personal Great American Novel, if you will. We decide (for the most part) what the plot will be, who the characters are—and we alone can hit the "delete" key. It often isn't the grand experience that ends up contributing the most to our work; it is the common, everyday experiences that add up to an interesting and fulfilling life.

Today I will notice the small things around me that make my life more pleasant and meaningful.

Let it Shine!

"Don't live down to expectations. Go out there and do something remarkable."
Wendy Wasserstein

───

*L*iving the less-than life is the easiest thing in the world, while becoming remarkable is incredibly difficult. It means putting ourselves out there and letting ourselves be vulnerable. Sharing our gifts with others can be like undressing in front of a roomful of respected peers: absolutely terrifying! But can you imagine what the world would be like if we all stopped holding ourselves back and lived our best lives? What amazing inventions, what art there would be if we each lived up to our full potential!

Today I will take a chance and share a talent with others.

Do It Anyway

"Is the goal distant, and troubled the road,
And the way long?
And heavy your load?
Then gird up your courage, and say 'I am strong,'
And keep going."

Ella Wheeler Wilcox

One of my favorite sayings is, "Do it anyway." What does this mean? Well, for starters, we all have a tough life at times. So what? Do we collapse by the side of the road and just give up? Of course not. In some small way, we "do it anyway" every single day.

My joints ache some days, but I still go about my day. Some months there's little money for groceries, but I still get creative and put food

on the table. I am nervous to make the call, but I still pick up the phone and inquire about that great freelance project I heard about. We all do difficult things, and each one makes us stronger.

Today I will tell myself, "I am strong; I can do hard things"—and I will really believe it!

Heart Exercises

"There is no better exercise for the heart than reaching down and lifting people up."

John Andrew Holmes Jr.

What a great mental picture: exercising our heart to help both ourselves *and* others! As we extend our hands and hearts toward others with love, something wonderful happens: Our own spirits become healed, our natures get refined, and our souls grow stronger. We become happier and more at peace. Try starting a new "exercise" program of loving kindness and service, and see how much good you can do for your own heart in the process.

Today I will be the one who reaches out to lift and help another.

Through a Child's Eyes

*"Cherishing children is the mark
of a civilized society."*

Joan Ganz Cooney

———

*N*othing pulls on the heartstrings more
than the sight of a child who is hungry
or hurting. Children are our future, and each

one has such potential. When any of them suffer, our hopes for the future—the future for all of us—dim a little.

Today I will reach out to help a child in need. Perhaps I will volunteer at my local children's hospital or at a homeless shelter that serves families with children.

Search in the Right Place

"The three grand essentials of happiness
are: something to do, someone to love,
and something to hope for."
Alexander Chalmers

I once heard a story about a man looking for his keys. He was on his hands and knees, searching the sidewalk under a streetlight when his friend saw him and offered to help him look. After more than an hour, his friend asked if he was *certain* this was where the keys were lost. "Oh no," said the man. "I lost them over there, in the dark under some bushes." Shocked, the friend asked why in the world he was looking for them in this spot, then. "Because the light is better here," said the man.

When it comes to our happiness, are we, like this man, looking in the wrong places? Things like wealth and pleasure glitter, but they are mere distractions. Lasting happiness is found through simpler things like fulfilling work and treasured time with loved ones.

Today I will think about what I can do, whom I can love, or what I might hope for that will contribute to my long-term happiness.

Rethinking "Failure"

*"Good people are good because they've
come to wisdom through failure."*
William Saroyan

___

Often, we don't get it right the first—or
even the hundredth—time. For most of us,
there is a whole lot of failure to wade through
before we reach success. But take heart—you
are in great company: Joan of Arc was rebuffed
by the first commander she approached about
joining the French Army. Thomas Edison made
more than 1,000 unsuccessful attempts before
he invented a practical lightbulb. And Walt
Disney was fired and even went bankrupt at
one point. Failing at something does not feel
good at the time, but failure and learning are
close companions. We gain wisdom through our
flops, and to someday get it right, we're going
to have to taste failure.

Today I will focus on what I am learning
through my setbacks, rather than focusing on
the setbacks themselves.

Letting Go

"I just lump everything in a great heap which I have labeled 'the past,' and, having thus emptied this deep reservoir that was once myself, I am ready to continue."
Zelda Fitzgerald

When I was young, I thought all things hurt or broken could be fixed: knees, bicycles, tea sets, feelings. One hard lesson of adulthood is that not everything can be repaired. Some things, well, you just have to *let them go*. It's easier said than done, but even the most difficult hurts from our past can, with determination, compassion, and hope for a better tomorrow, be left on the floor. After leaving them behind, we can walk forward with a lighter step and an unburdened heart.

Today I will face the new day with my gaze looking forward. I will not look back.

Rain, Rain—*Don't* Go Away!

"In those vernal seasons of the year when the air is calm and pleasant, it were an injury and sullenness against nature not to go out and see her riches, and partake in her rejoicing with heaven and earth."

John Milton

I live in the desert, and rain is such a novelty here, folks visiting from wetter places must think we locals are plum crazy for getting all worked up over a little rain! But, after day upon day of dry, unyielding heat, the rain—even a sprinkle—is such welcome relief. So, maybe it's not really so strange that nearly every time the sky opens up, we head outside instead of going in. Young girls break into impromptu dances, while little children sail tinfoil boats. It's one of our favorite ways to spend an afternoon.

When I go out today, I will be glad for the beauty of the season, whether it be rain, wind, sun, or snow.

Acting on Faith

"In a mood of faith and hope my work goes on. A ream of fresh paper lies on my desk waiting for the next book. I am a writer and I take up my pen to write."

Pearl S. Buck

From time to time, we all act on faith, even if we don't recognize it as such. Would a farmer plant his fields if he did not expect to reap a harvest in due time? Would a student attend classes and study if she did not believe it would further her life and career? Would we get up and go to work each day if we did not hope that by doing so we would accomplish something? Perhaps if we tap into faith more often and more deliberately, we will be moved to act with more purpose and conviction.

Today I will act upon something I believe in, even if I cannot yet see the end result.

Work with a Purpose

"Set me a task in which I can put something of my very self, and it is a task no longer; it is joy; it is art."

Bliss Carman

After my first child was born, I quit my job to stay home full-time. During the first months, I had moments when I felt like my intellect and some of my talents were being wasted. I longed to do something creative. At some point, though, my outlook shifted, and I came to the realization that you can find meaning in and "put something of yourself" into any task—including child

care and housework. I try to look at the chores before me each day not merely as endless busywork, but as steps to providing a peaceful, orderly sanctuary where love, learning, and happiness can thrive.

Today I will try to find a way to put something of my very self into every task.

Bulking Up for What Lies Ahead

"You have to accept whatever comes, and the only important thing is that you meet it with the best you have to give."

Eleanor Roosevelt

*M*isfortune is no respecter of persons. Trouble and hardship do not discriminate. Face it—misfortune is bound to happen to each of us. If we accept that adversity will happen, we can decide, here and now, to face it with as much courage and optimism as we can muster. Often we don't think much about how we will handle adversity until it is upon us. But much like a

muscle that strengthens with use, we can "bulk up" our optimism and our courage to prepare in advance for how we will face—and conquer—the challenges that lie ahead.

Today I will spend time exercising my optimism muscle! I will give every challenge my best effort.

The Worth of a Person

"Every individual matters. Every individual has a role to play. Every individual makes a difference."

Jane Goodall

$\mathcal{O}$ne of my family's favorite movies is *It's a Wonderful Life*. The premise of the film has been copied and parodied time and time again: that is, take one person out of existence, and all sorts of seemingly unrelated things unravel. The timeless moral is that each life, however average or seemingly

insignificant, matters. What would be different if you hadn't been born? Who would be worse off if you weren't here today? There is no way to really measure the far-reaching effects of one life, but it's an eye-opening idea to ponder.

Today I will be aware of the weight and significance of my life and my role to play here on earth, and I will play it well.

The Happiness Factor

"If only we'd stop trying to be happy
we'd have a pretty good time."
Edith Wharton

I remember my grandmother saying now and again that happiness was irrelevant. I didn't understand what she meant back then, but I get it now. Happiness is elusive. The more we aim for it, the more we fall short of it. The more we try to imitate others who are "happy," the worse we feel. We need to find our own joy by waking up and making the decision to

have a happy day, and then going about our daily activities without giving happiness another thought. We can find more genuine joy in life if we focus instead on relationships and finding meaning in our lives, rather than in finding happiness.

Today I will be present in the moment. I will focus intently on each task and commitment, and today will be a happy day for me.

Seize the Day

"Great opportunities come to all, but many do not know they have met them. The only preparation to take advantage of them is single fidelity to watch what each day brings."

Albert E. Dunning

*M*ost of us are expert procrastinators; I know I am. If you are anything like me, you can think of numerous things to do to get you out of the task at hand. We worry for days (or weeks, or longer!) about something that, in the end, takes only a few hours to finish. Maybe if we can focus on the satisfaction and relief of finally getting a procrastinated task done, we will be quicker to jump in and do it the next time.

Today I will pick one thing I have been putting off, and I will get started on it.

Growth from Work

"All growth depends upon activity. There is no development physically or intellectually without effort, and effort means work. Work is not a curse; it is...the measure of civilization."

Calvin Coolidge

Stress-free living is not the path to happiness some psychologists and yoga gurus would have us believe. For if we are completely stress-free at all times, even of "good stress," we are likely not doing very much. That kind of stagnation can have ill effects after a while. Our brains (our frontal lobes, to be exact) crave frequent activity to keep us happy. Serotonin and endorphins—the body's natural feel-good chemicals—flood our systems when we rush to meet a deadline or make an important decision. Work is not only a necessity of life, it is something that will help us enjoy life. That is not to say that we should always run on all cylinders, of course! Moderation is the key in everything.

Today I will value my work, and I will take note of the longer-term goals it helps accomplish.

Generation to Generation

"We should so live and labor in our time that what came to us as seed may go to the next generation as blossom, and that which came to us as blossom may go to them as fruit. That is what we mean by progress."

Henry Ward Beecher

*E*very generation advances on the knowledge of the generation that preceded it. This is a gift and a responsibility. Did the generation before us leave us with a lot to work with? Certainly. Did the generation before us also leave us with a lot to work on? Indeed. We must use the gifts we were given to work on the issues we now face. This is both a challenge and an opportunity, and the next generation will judge us on it.

As I work today, I will be thankful to those who came before me, and mindful of the fact that I am responsible to those who come after me.

Laughter, the Best Medicine

*"Life is far too important a thing
ever to talk seriously about."*

Oscar Wilde

———

There is a time and place for taking things seriously, but many of us are far too serious, far too much of the time. Life can get pretty stressful with all its bills, work deadlines, health problems, worries about the future—the list goes on and on and is specific to each one of us. Faced with such unrelenting stress, sometimes the best thing to do is laugh. Finding the humor in life is a powerful antidote to stress and worry. Nothing works faster to bring your mind and body back into balance than a good laugh.

Today I will go out to a comedy club or watch a favorite funny movie—one that I know is guaranteed to make me laugh out loud!

Appreciating All Talents

"The worst form of inequality is to try to make unequal things equal."

Aristotle

A lot of us are wary of competition these days. For instance, many adults resist keeping score in children's game play or sporting events out of fear of hurting a child's feelings. The hard truth is, though, that "sparing" our children in this way often only leads to delayed and increased upset. Most children are much more resilient than we give them credit for. Let them lose. If you show them that it is no big deal, they will be okay with it. Competition is a good thing. It gives us an idea of where we are succeeding and what we need to work on. There will always be someone who's better at a given task. When we marvel at the talents of others as well as appreciate our own, we all win.

Today I will congratulate someone else on their talent, but I will not allow someone else's triumph to lead me to devalue my own gifts.

What We Want Versus What We Need

"I can never read all the books I want; I can never be all the people I want and live all the lives I want. I can never train myself in all the skills I want. And why do I want? I want to live and feel all the shades, tones and variations of mental and physical experience possible in life."

Sylvia Plath

*D*o you ever think, *I wonder what it would be like to be a doctor* (or a teacher, or a photographer, or any job other than your current job)? We cannot lead all the lives we dream about, but we can add as many exciting details to our lives as possible.

If we daydream of being a doctor but our job is a teacher, what is it about the life of a doctor that makes us daydream about it? That we could be helpful in a life-threatening situation? We could get a taste of that in our own life by getting certified in CPR and being ready to assist if we were ever to witness an accident or other traumatic situation. There is always room to enhance our lives by adding to our skill sets.

Today I will sign up for a class in a subject I've always daydreamed about. In this way I will be adding to my skill set.

Give and Take

"It is an eternal obligation toward the human being not to let him suffer from hunger when one has a chance of coming to his assistance."
Simone Weil

Every day most of us come into contact with someone who is suffering, and it usually gives us an empty feeling in the middle of our being. Helping others helps them, of course, but it also helps us. We get a feeling of accomplishment and a sense of community. We know that at times we have been and will again be the recipient of others' help, whether in the form of a lead on a job, a visit when we were grieving, or a helping hand when we were on a tight deadline. Community works best when this give and take is in smooth, constant motion.

Today I will be ready to give if called upon, and I will also be ready to take if I am in need. I will be an active participant in my community.

Love Wins

"I have found the paradox, that if you love until it hurts, there can be no more hurt, only more love."

Mother Teresa

*L*oving puts us in a vulnerable position. Whether it's romantic love or the love of a parent, child, or friend, choosing to love involves risk.

We can get hurt by being rejected, by having to watch our loved one suffer, or by losing our loved one. If we endure through the hurt, though, we will be rewarded with the truth that love always wins.

We may get rejected or we may get hurt, but if we cling to love, we win. Hold fast to love through any hurt, and you will eventually find yourself no longer feeling any pain because love has overtaken the hurt and only the love remains. The only way to end up losing is to never love out of fear of being hurt or to allow ourselves to be overtaken by bitterness after rejection or loss. If we stay on the side of love, we win.

Today I will cling to love—no matter what.

Try, Try Again

"In every triumph there's a lot of try."
Frank Tyger

"If at first you don't succeed, try, try again."
My Dad used to say that all the time.
It sometimes drove me crazy! But little by

little, it seeped into my subconscious until it became a part of who I am. Now, I tell my own kids the same thing. It probably drives them crazy too, but I know that someday they will appreciate the advice.

Today I will not give up. If something is too difficult, I will take a few deep breaths, square my shoulders, and try again.

Growing Older and Loving It!

"I have found it to be true that the older I've become the better my life has become."
Doris Lessing

Many elements of our culture prod us to fear aging: *Oh, no! I will get lines on my face! I won't be able to get around and be as active as I like.* Most of us, though, have loved ones who are elderly, and it is not unusual for them to be running around like much younger people. The key is to take care of yourself as best you can and to *be okay with aging!* Why are we so scared? We should feel that life is expanding, not contracting. Aging is a natural part of life. Take care of yourself, keep smiling, and relish and add to your store of memories. The secret to aging with grace is to fill our days with creativity, relationships, and purpose.

Today I will identify three ways in which my life is better today than it was even a few years ago.

Radiate Peace

"Every time we hold our tongues instead of returning the sharp retort, show patience with another's faults, show a little more love and kindness, we are helping to stock-pile more of these peace-bringing qualities in the world instead of armaments for war."

Constance Foster

$\mathcal{P}$atience is requested of most of us numerous times throughout any given day. As we commute to work—whether we walk, ride a bike, drive, or take the train or bus—we are asked at times to yield to others, while at other times, others show patience and yield to us. Throughout our day we can choose to act with love and promote peace, or we can choose to be selfish and look out only for ourselves. We know in our hearts which choice promotes peace. The more we choose the peaceful route, the more we make peace radiate all around us.

Today I will show my support for patience, love, and peace at every opportunity.

Beauty in Every Season

"Nature gives to every time and season some beauties of its own."
Charles Dickens

I live in Arizona, where desert summers often send temperatures soaring above 100 degrees. It can be hard to remember the beauties of the season when you feel like your legs are melted to the car seat! And yet, the sunsets this time of year are awe-inspiring. And the summer lightning shows take my breath away. If I wake up early enough, I can walk before the heat becomes too much and see the hummingbirds on the blooming cactus flowers, watch the clouds change shape in the endless blue sky, and, if I'm lucky, even catch a glimpse of a roadrunner. When I take the time to be quiet and attentive, summer in the desert fills me up with joy.

Today I will look past the difficulties to find the beauty in whatever place and season in which I find myself.

Keep Truth Alive

"Truth is the only safe ground to stand upon."
Elizabeth Cady Stanton

*O*ne of the easiest ways to simplify our lives is to make a decision to always be truthful. Sometimes it is tempting to fudge the truth, and then to tell a little lie, and before we know it, things are all befuddled. Giving honest answers to begin with always keeps things simpler. Sometimes we fudge the truth because we don't want circumstances to reflect

badly on us or we don't want to hurt someone or get someone else in trouble. The safest course, though, is to simply give an accurate account of what happened. Things can always be worked out, and it's easier to work them out right away instead of confusing the situation with inaccurate information.

Today I will show that I value the truth by being honest in all of my interactions with others.

The Power Inside Us

"Nothing splendid has ever been achieved except by those who dared believe that something inside them was superior to circumstance."

Bruce Barton

*W*e are all superior to our circumstances because we all have limitless potential. We can break free from any circumstance by saying, "How can I achieve this dream of mine?" If we want something badly enough, we can use our brains and our talents to find a way to make our dream a reality. While some

people bow to life's challenges, we all know or have heard of folks who seem to succeed in spite of health challenges, poverty, addiction, or any number of other difficult circumstances. Success is possible if you believe in it and keep going.

Today I will fight for my dreams.

From Maddening to Marveling

"In all things there is something of the marvelous."

Aristotle

*M*any of us lead such busy lives that we rarely take the time to appreciate the beauty and wonder all around us. Even the tiniest or seemingly ugliest things are amazing if we take the time to consider them. Ponder ants, for instance. They drive us crazy when their armies get into our houses and march around as if they own the place, but their tenacity and industriousness are impressive—especially for such tiny creatures. Use this tactic with anything that drives you nuts over the course of your day, and you will have your mind wandering toward marveling.

If I am confronted by something maddening today, I will find a way to marvel instead.

Work Therapy

"The days you work are the best days."
Georgia O'Keeffe

---

*W*hat Ms. O'Keeffe probably didn't know is that there is a bevy of scientific, psychological, and medical research standing behind her statement. Numerous recent studies show that work is good for both your physical and mental health. Making a contribution to society through working boosts our self-esteem and brings confidence and security into our lives. Work can help you recover from illness and injury and can even ward off aging. So while we may dream of sipping a piña colada in the sun somewhere, it's really a good day's work that keeps us healthy and happy!

As I go about my daily tasks today, I will tap into that good feeling of being productive and constructive.

306

Steering Our Course

*"It is our relation to circumstances that
determines their influence over us.
The same wind that carries one vessel into
port may blow another off shore."*

Christian Bovée

o you see challenges as opportunities or
calamities? Let's say you are assigned a
project at work and it is a doozy—a real mess.
Do you dive right in and do your best, or do
you collapse in your chair, defeated before you
even begin? Don't let yourself be overwhelmed—
ride your challenge into port and relish the
congratulatory applause that awaits!

**Today I will rise to every challenge I face with
a positive outlook.**

Living Your Values

"The greatest way to live with honor in this world is to be what we pretend to be."

Socrates

he way we see ourselves does not always jibe with the way others see us. Sometimes this is because we do not take the time to really examine ourselves. What are the traits you most value and most want to exhibit in your life? Generosity? Kindness? Hard work? Take stock of your activities and conversations from time to time, and make sure they match your values.

Today I will write a journal entry and include all the important events and discussions of the day. I will be honest with myself, and if I am disappointed in any regard, I will do better tomorrow.

Creating Truth

"Our truest responsibility to the irrationality of the world is to paint or sing or write, for only in such response do we find the truth."
Madeleine L'Engle

*D*o you see yourself as an artist? For years, I didn't. Then, little by little, I gave in to little yearnings to create. Now I see that I am a very creative person. Moreover, I am continually affected by the beauty and power of the works others create. Each time I am touched by the words of a favorite poem, moved by a beautiful song, inspired

by a photograph, transported by a fresh culinary creation, or amazed by a new technology, I feel I have been given a little nugget of truth. Each truth adds to the knowledge and inspiration that came before it and helps me see the world in a new—and wonderful—way.

Today I will contribute to truth by creating something new.

Background Music

"Music is a moral law. It gives soul to the universe, wings to the mind, flight to the imagination, and charm and gaiety to life and to everything."

Plato

I love to have music playing in the background as I write, drive, or do chores around the house. Music isn't a distraction the way television can be. I seem to just take it in as I do other things, instead of having to give it my complete attention. And I reap so much from it! It soothes my mind and my soul, and I feel like it helps me perform better at my tasks because I feel so soothed and at peace.

Today I will expand my horizons by listening to a genre of music that is not very familiar to me.

Consult with Yourself

"Let me listen to me and not to them."
Gertrude Stein

~

When we open the floodgates, we
sometimes let too many opinions pull us

this way and that. What we need to learn to do is get in tune with our own inner voice, for it is the only one that really matters. What do you want? What do you want to accomplish? What is important to you? Take time every week to consult with yourself.

Today I will take the time to consult with myself, and I will do my own bidding.

Revise Away!

"It's never too late, in fiction or in life, to revise."
Nancy Thayer

~⚓~

Regret holds us back. It is unproductive. If you have regrets, start revising! If

you have regrets over something you failed to do, do it now! Maybe you fear you "missed your chance," but you can always have another (at least similar) one.

Let's say you regret quitting at something. Take it up again. Maybe you quit a sport when you were younger, or you quit a job and always wondered where it might have led. Take up the

activity again in any way you can. It may be too late to chase your dream of being a professional tennis player, but you can join a local league and play once a week. If your chief regret is something you did do but wish you hadn't done, make amends however you can and rewrite the ending to that chapter of your life. It is never too late.

Today I will pick some area of my life that I would like to revise, and I will get to work.

We Need Each Other

once heard a story about a farmer whose fruit won awards at the State Fair year after year. He had guarded his secret closely,

letting others speculate on whether it was the soil, special additives, or expensive seeds that made his fruit so good. One year he decided to finally reveal the secret to his prize-winning crops. "I've been giving my seeds away for years," he said. The farmer explained how his crops couldn't grow so well in isolation; they had to be cross-pollinated. Therefore the better his neighbors' crops were, the better his crops were too.

This lesson can apply to human communities as well. It is in our best interests for our neighbors to thrive, as it lifts up our whole community. When we look out for and support each other, we all benefit.

Today I will engage in an activity that will benefit my community and me. Perhaps I will sign up to volunteer at my local school, library, or museum.

Forgive Someone Today

"Forgiveness is a virtue of the brave."
Indira Gandhi

⌐

*F*orgiveness isn't an emotion or feeling.
If we wait until we "feel like" forgiving
someone who has wronged us, that day may

never come. And who do we think is suffering while we wait? We are. Holding on to negative emotions only hurts us; the one who did us wrong is most likely sleeping through the night just fine! No, forgiveness is an act, a decision, a choice—and one each of us can make this very day!

Today I will make the choice to forgive someone who has wronged me.

The Open Air

"Set wide the window. Let me drink the day."
Edith Wharton

The tidy tract home I grew up in faced
what seemed to me acres of raw land.
Never mind that
it was still very
much within the
city—it was my
own intimate
wilderness, and I
remember being
very happy there.
My friends and
I collected rocks,
chased lizards, and
played hide-and-
seek and capture

the flag until long after the sun went down. My love of the outdoors was forged in the brush-covered vacant lots of my childhood, and this love continues to the present moment.

Today I will set aside time to wander in a place where I can breathe and think in the open air.

Make Others Happy

"Do not run after happiness, but seek to do good, and you will find that happiness will run after you."

James Freeman Clarke

A few years ago I started a tradition for my birthday. Instead of hoping for gifts and attention, I took my birthday

happiness in my own hands and spent the day giving others "gifts"—one for each year of my life. This year with my two daughters as my dates, we crisscrossed the city doing I-won't-tell-you-how-many random acts of kindness. They were just simple things: mowing our elderly neighbor's lawn, adding coins to expired meters, picking up garbage at the park, delivering travel-size personal items to a homeless shelter, passing out a few movie gift cards at the mall, and handing out flowers to residents of a nursing home. As the day ended, I was overflowing with happiness. It was the best birthday I have ever had.

Today I will plan a day where I will focus not on what will make me happy but on spending the day devoted to the happiness of a loved one who has been having a rough time. I will put the day in my planner and hold myself accountable to deliver!

Today Deserves Our Full Attention

"We know nothing of tomorrow; our business is to be good and happy today."
Sydney Smith

I often find myself worrying about tomorrow, or next week, or next month, or next year. It is futile, when you think about it; all we can do is plan to do our best today, for any number of things can happen before tomorrow comes. In the meantime, if I spend too much time focused on the future, I will miss out on the many moments I could be treasuring today.

Today my thoughts and efforts will be focused on the here and now. I will not get ahead of myself or spend too much time in dreamland.

The Work of Love

"Love is a verb."

Clare Boothe Luce

We are bombarded with ideas about love throughout any given day. We see billboards for romantic movies, ads for romantic gifts, posts about romantic troubles—the list goes on.

The fact of the matter is, though, that although our culture portrays love in dreamy ways that are all about us, true love involves work and effort that benefits another. If we love our child, we put forth extra effort for him or her; we soothe him when he is upset even if it puts us behind schedule on a hectic morning. If we love our parent, we go the extra mile for him or her as well; when our mother calls us at work, we lovingly listen, even if she seems to be rambling and we are on a tight deadline. And if we truly love our spouse or significant other, we show them how we feel in some small way every day, whether by forgiving an errant sock on the floor or making time for him or her when they really seem to need it, even though we might feel like having some "me time." Yes, love is work—glorious, fulfilling work that no one can sub for.

Today I will do many works of love, and I will put my heart into it.

The Pursuit of Happiness

*M*any of us fall into the trap of thinking too much. We spend our time comparing ourselves to others, and we fret if we come to the conclusion that we don't "measure up." The trick is not to measure, for what are we measuring, anyway? Every life is different. We may look at another and think, *If I traveled as often as she does, then I would be happy.* Or, *If my family had as much money as they do, we'd be happier.* These types of thoughts don't get us anywhere. If we think about it and take stock, there are probably plenty of things about our lives that could make us happy—we just have to choose to be so and move on with our lives.

Today I will choose happiness. I will not overthink it—I will just be happy!

The Power of Play

"You can discover more about a person in an hour of play than in a year of conversation."
Plato

*M*y extended family gets together a few times a year. I always look forward to these gatherings because there's so much to

catch up on. Yet last year I was surprised by how little we actually had to say to each other! We were all gathered in this nice, comfortable room, but we found ourselves just looking at each other. I racked my mind for things to talk about, but like old friends, we'd heard it all before. After someone suggested venturing over to the nearby beach for a game of volleyball, however, things got really interesting! I had no idea how talented some of my family members were (or how clumsy I was!). We had a blast

and lots of laughs. I have already started planning activities for next year's gathering.

Today I will think of a fun activity I haven't done in a while, and I will invite a friend to join me.

The Tortoise Still Beats the Hare

"As long as the day lasts, let's give it all we got."
David O. McKay

A s exhausting as it can be, there is simply no substitute for hard work. Talent can't replace it, nor can good luck; neither intelligence nor power can make up for a lack of hard work. The beautiful thing about hard work is that anyone can apply it. The application of hard work over time increases our accomplishments. The fact is, the person who has little natural ability but is consistently diligent will eventually run circles around the one who is gifted but lazy.

Today I will give my best effort on every task.

Your Own Path

"Follow your own path,
no matter what people say."
Karl Marx

~

Sometimes it can seem easier to follow
the advice of others, especially if you
are feeling unsure of yourself. It is at times

like these that it helps to take a moment to yourself to meditate on what feels right to you, deep down. Whether you are making a big decision on what path to follow in your career, or a small decision about what to wear, be true to yourself. Follow your heart, do what you love, know your own style.

Today I will listen to my heart, not to outside advice. I will follow my own path.

I Will Try

"You may be whatever you resolve to be.
Determine to be something in the world, and you
will be something. 'I cannot,' never accomplished
anything: 'I will try,' has wrought wonders."

Joel Hawes

As a young man, my grandfather contracted polio. The doctors told him he would never walk again, but he vowed to walk out of that hospital on his own two feet. With hard work and determination, he did just that. He went on to serve in the U.S. Navy in World War II and to dance with his future wife, my grandmother, when he met her at a USO dance while in port. He never accepted "cannot" but instead insisted "I can." As an old man, he walks with a cane, but he has lived a long and vigorous life. He became who he wanted to be despite the odds. Determination has indeed wrought wonders.

As I approach difficult tasks today, I will face them with a determined, "I can do this" attitude.

A Magic Vase

*"Life is a magic vase filled to the brim;
so made that you cannot dip into it nor draw
from it; but it overflows into the hand that drops
treasures into it—drop in malice and it overflows
hate; drop in charity and it overflows love."*

John Ruskin

Every time I garden, life reminds me of the wonders it offers; every new bloom is a treasure, life renewing itself like magic. A garden responds to the caretaking of the gardener—weeding, pruning, watering. The love and care you put into it yields results, as in life. Nurture and care for the people and places (schools, community centers) in your town, and the people blossom in response. You can't make the magic happen just by wanting it, you have to add something to that magic vase. Become a docent at the zoo, plant a butterfly garden in your yard, help kids paint a colorful wall mural in the community, or volunteer to teach someone to read. The possibilities for magic are endless.

Today I will bring magic into life.

Commitment

*"Individual commitment to a group effort—
that is what makes a team work, a company
work, a society work, a civilization work."*
Vince Lombardi

Anyone who has had to ask for help
knows that it isn't all about "me."
Individual accomplishments are admirable,
but we can accomplish far more when we
work together. Schools can be built, charities
can be organized, bridges can be designed
and constructed, and community gardens can
be enjoyed by generations to come. It is to
those teams, from small committees to large
communities, that we owe our thanks.

**Today I will reach out and join a group or
team—whether a local book group or a village
board meeting—and I will contribute.**

Give Until It Hurts

"She broke the bread into two fragments,
and gave them to the children,
who ate with avidity. 'She has kept none
for herself,' grumbled the sergeant.
'Because she is not hungry,' said a soldier.
'Because she is a mother,' said the sergeant."

Victor Hugo

*P*arents know what it means
to give until it hurts—but
it's a good hurt. Your children are
more precious than any fortune,
you would give anything to help
them, and their happiness is your
happiness. In the same way, teachers,
nurses, soup kitchen volunteers,
firefighters, and so many others find

happiness in giving to others. And when an ordinary mother—or the extraordinary Mother Teresa—feeds the hungry, it inspires us all. Such selfless caring and compassion can be an example to us in our daily lives.

Today I will look for opportunities to help others, and I will find happiness in giving.

Of Journals and Memories

*"Nothing has really happened
until it has been recorded."*
Virginia Woolf

—⚜—

If something is forgotten, did it ever really happen? This question keeps me writing in my journal every day, for I don't want to lose a single precious memory. In the past it has been maddening to me when I've enjoyed a wonderful journey but—when asked about it— could not give many details because I had not kept a journal. And these days it is so easy! We can have our own private blog and quickly type away; we can even upload pictures in just minutes. Though detailed entries in a simple paper journal still do the trick as well. There are few excuses that hold water anymore.

Before I go to bed tonight, I will add to my journal, even if I write just one simple sentence.

I Love This World

"We live in this world when we love it."
Rabindranath Tagore

It is easy to sit on the sidelines and fret about all that's wrong with the world. The stronger and more productive tactic, though, is to take the world for what it is—the good and the bad—and make a conscious choice to love it and be engaged. Find what is good in it, and cling to that. Fight to make the rest of it better. If we just sit on the sidelines and fret, we are part of the problem instead of being part of the solution.

I love this world, for better or for worse, and I choose to fight for what is good in it every single day.

When We Give,
We Also Gain

*"There is a wonderful mythical law of nature
that the three things we crave most in life—
happiness, freedom and peace of mind—are
always attained by giving them to someone else."*
Peyton Conway March

We win by giving away. It boggles the mind and perhaps seems even too good to be true, but I think, if most of us look back on our lives, we can see the truth of this statement. When I am generous and try to give a little happiness to someone else—say, by donating items to a homeless shelter—I gain something for myself as well. I obviously come away with a good feeling because I know I have likely touched someone's life; I can feel good about myself for that. But I also gain a sense of community. I know others are not alone, and it helps me realize that I am not alone either. If I help someone achieve freedom by tutoring at a prison or donating money to a charity that helps victims of slavery worldwide, again, I also gain something because it helps me value my own freedoms more. If I give peace of mind to another by forgiving them for a past hurt, I free myself by leaving the conflict in the past and moving on to a free future. Truly when we give, we also gain.

I will find a way to give to someone else today, and after I do, I will reflect on how it has enhanced my own life as well.

Be in the Way Sometimes

"You can't achieve anything without getting in someone's way. You can't be detached and effective."

Abba Eban

Sometimes it is tempting to live on the periphery of life because that way there is less stress and conflict. We are each better than that type of life, though. Yes, if we interact with others, we may sometimes butt heads and may sometimes even get our feelings hurt. We should not let such minor concerns hold us back, though. Each of us has a lot to offer, something valuable to say and contribute.

Interacting with others can sometimes be wonderful; at other times, it can be less than wonderful. As long as we are respectful, we are doing our part. We can't control the behavior of others. At times they will act as though we are getting in their way. If they react that way, we should respectfully remind them that we can achieve more if we work together.

If I have issues interacting with others today, I will not let it bother me. I will be respectful, but I will also be undeterred.

We Are Always Ourselves

"We are always the same age inside."
Gertrude Stein

*F*retting about age must be one of the silliest wastes of time there is. For we really are always the same age on the inside, aren't we? We are always ourselves. Our inner voice has not changed that much—it has simply become wiser. I am now considered middle-aged, but I am still me. It is a sad thing to value yourself less because of a few wrinkles. I wear my wrinkles and scars with pride. I have earned them!

Today I will not spend a single thought or second engaged in fretting over age. My age is my badge of honor.

357

Getting Along with Others

*"Having two bathrooms ruined
the capacity to co-operate."*
Margaret Mead

These days, some of our lives are easy and separate almost to the point of being ridiculous. Many single people live alone even if they struggle to afford it because living with others drives them crazy. Some people send elderly parents to nursing homes rather than taking them into their own homes even when their health does not necessitate nursing-home care. Some married couples have separate bedrooms to guarantee each person their own space. To each their own, of course, but there is something to be said for learning the skills necessary to compromise and work things out with others. Often compromise leads to collaboration, and wonderful things can come from that.

If an opportunity for compromise or collaboration comes along today, I will jump right in the mix and see what evolves.

Doing Our Personal Best

"Never mind what others do; do better than yourself, beat your own record from day to day, and you are a success."
William J. H. Boetcker

Something I've always liked about the sport of swimming is that you don't simply "win" or "lose" at the end of a race. Of course there's a winner, but additionally, each individual swimmer records their own individual time, and from week to week each tries to best their "PR" (personal record). In life, it is good to focus on being your own best self and try to improve in increments day by day. The accomplishments or activities of others really have little to do with your own progress. Life isn't a race in which you are competing against other people. Everyone's "race" is a unique journey full of adventures and challenges.

Today I will improve my PR in one area of my life.

Wisdom Thrives in Silence

"Much wisdom often goes with fewer words."

Sophocles

My dad was not a big talker. He was a man of action, even after retirement. He was always busy doing something in the yard or in the house. When he did talk, though, people listened because he usually had something interesting to say. He just didn't believe in talking unless he had something important to offer. I think this goes hand in hand with simplicity. He lived a fairly simple life; he liked to keep things uncomplicated. Life does not have to be complicated, and it needs few words, really. If we live simply whenever possible, we can leave the extra time and words to the issues that need them.

Today I will live simply and give my mouth the day off except for when words are absolutely necessary.

Don't Be a Cynic

*"Don't be a cynic, and bewail and bemoan.
Omit the negative propositions. Don't waste
yourself in rejection, nor bark against the
bad, but chant the beauty of the good."*

Ralph Waldo Emerson

Being a cynic is easy. All you have to do is sit there and point out all the ways in which everyone else is wrong. Yes, many things are wrong in the world, but that is because they are the best attempts *so far*. They are not proven methods, but at least they are attempts. The cynic sees no point in even making an attempt because he fears failure.

I do not want to be a cynic. I want to be a doer. I know that means I will face failure, but if I fail, I will simply move on. All my efforts are just my best attempts—and my attempts will continue to get better and better until at last I succeed.

Today if I find myself getting discouraged, I will call to mind all that is right, good, and beautiful in my life, and I will move on.

Give a Little of Yourself

"No fine work can be done without concentration and self-sacrifice and toil and doubt."

Max Beerbohm

*L*ife takes concentration, self-sacrifice, toil, and doubt. If we think back over the times we have most needed these qualities, we will probably call to mind our greatest works. Every worthy task demands these qualities. If we don't have to concentrate, we can be sure we aren't doing anything very difficult. If we

never sacrifice ourselves, we aren't doing anything of significance. And if we never doubt, we aren't taking our responsibilities seriously enough. In fact, we know a work is good if we know exactly where or when we gave a little of ourselves to it.

Today I will endeavor to work hard, give a little of myself, and fight through any doubt. If I do a little of all three today, I can rest assured that I am making progress.

Give Without Keeping Track

"That's what I consider true generosity.
You give your all, and yet you always
feel as if it costs you nothing."
Simone de Beauvoir

When we are asked to contribute in life, do we jot down our contribution? Do we "keep track," if you will? Do we say, "Well, I helped Sally out today, but if she asks again before helping me first, I will say no the next time"? This is not the nature of true generosity, is it? True, if we don't keep track, we risk giving more than we get in return. There is always the real risk of being taken advantage of or giving so much to others that there's little left for ourselves or for our closest loved ones. But, at least once in a while, give without keeping track or expecting anything in return. It will leave you with a calm, peaceful, weightless feeling.

Today I will give with no expectations.

Love Empowers

"Love makes your soul crawl out
from its hiding place."
Zora Neale Hurston

Love is a freeing thing. If we were lucky enough to experience unconditional love as children, this comes as no surprise. When we feel loved, we feel anchored, and this helps give us courage. If we first experience this feeling during adulthood, our eyes are opened and we see ourselves as the unique creatures we are.

If we have had trouble receiving this love from others, we can make the empowering decision to love ourselves and set ourselves free. It is a paradox of life that it is easier to love those who seem to love themselves, while it is hard to love oneself until we feel loved by others. Make the choice every day to act in a loving way toward yourself, for that is where love begins.

Today I will love with no limits. I will choose to love my soul, and I will release it to experience the wonder of the world.

Liking What You Do

*"Doing what you like is freedom.
Liking what you do is happiness."*
Frank Tyger

It's a blessed and lucky thing to love what you do and earn a living at the same time. For most of us, the two may not come into perfect alignment. Should we therefore grump and gripe about how things are not perfect? Why wait for circumstances to be perfect before we will be happy? It's up to us to choose to be happy and to find the joy in what we do each day. Bypass all the complaints and set aside any grievances about what we cannot change for now, and go straight to the happiness.

Today I will explore what I like best about what I do, and I will be happy.

Simple Indulgences

"There must be quite a few things a hot bath won't cure, but I don't know many of them."

Sylvia Plath

We all feel the need to luxuriate every once in a while. After a long day at work, or a harried day watching over the kids (or both!), indulge and renew yourself! Even if you are just feeling a little bit down, treating yourself to something special helps to remind you that you are valuable and special— just for being you! What is your favorite thing? A soapy soak as

in the above quote, an hour alone at the library or coffee shop, or a serene and peacefully solitary walk in the woods? Take a moment to consider what you most long for right now—and make that a gift to yourself.

Today I will treat myself to something special.

Truth Leads to Originality

"Truth is the nursing mother of genius.
No man can be absolutely true to himself,
eschewing cant, compromise, servile imitation,
and complaisance without becoming original."
Margaret Fuller

The most brilliant figures in history were original. Think of inventor Albert Einstein with his wild hair. Or George Sand, a female writer in early 19th-century France, rejecting the social mores of her time by wearing pants.

Such figures as these were both brilliant and original because they were true to themselves. By thinking independently, they were able to tap into their creativity and determine for themselves what was important to them—whether choosing science over hair care, or the practicality of pants at a time when all other women wore dresses. So, too, in our own more ordinary lives can we be true to ourselves, and—just perhaps—tap into our own genius!

Today I will look into my own heart and be true to myself.

Making a Life

"I've learned that making a 'living' is not the same thing as making a 'life.'"

Maya Angelou

*T*here's more to life than work; on some level, we all know this is true. But in our day-to-day lives, we often put so much of our esteem into our work that there are days when it may seem as though our work is our whole life. While the value of work is a good thing, it's home we always return to; this is where our loved ones are, where we build the history of family generations and provide a sanctuary where we nurture the future. From this safe place we launch the lives we really want to lead, and only part of that is bringing home a paycheck.

378

Some are lucky and can parlay their business into accomplishing a life dream, but for many of us, making a living is a means to an end—not the end itself. While we appreciate the stability of work, let's make our "daily work " be building a life worth living.

Today I will contemplate the elements of my ideal life and work to make that dream come true.

Assume the Best Intentions

"The growth of wisdom may be gauged
accurately by the decline of ill temper."
Friedrich Wilhelm Nietzsche

$\smile$

$\mathcal{S}$ ome years ago, I moved from a big city—
which offered public transportation—
out to the suburbs, where I needed to drive

a car to get around. It wasn't long before I discovered I had a temper quick to respond to being cut off, or tailgated, or any other of a number of driving irritations. Hello, road rage. My friends and family soon noticed my bad mood after every commute, and I realized that I was creating my own unhappiness.

Then one day I was driving home from the pet store with a new guppy bound for my fish tank, taking it slowly, driving gingerly over the railroad tracks. When other drivers responded

with honking, I realized that no one really knows what another person is experiencing, and instead of anger, it would be wiser to reserve judgment and respond with compassion and calm. Goodbye, road rage! Whether driving, negotiating a crowded store, or dealing with a telemarketing call, it's good to assume the best intentions and respect others' feelings and experiences.

Today, when faced with a frustrating situation, I will take a deep breath, assume the best in others, and let go of anger.

Doing Our Duty

"Not only is there a right to be happy, there is a duty to be happy. So much sadness exists in the world that we are all under obligation to contribute as much joy as lies within our powers."

John S. Bonnell

What would the world look like if everyone felt an obligation to be happy? What if we responded to those we meet with positivity instead of negativity? What if we all felt it was our shared responsibility to humanity to contribute happiness? One can hardly imagine the increase in prosperity, peace, and joy!

Today I will act as if happiness were my duty.